MW00777452

# Grown Sexy Wisdom

## 5 Grown Ass Ways to Create a Life that Turns You ON!

### By: Lianna Gardner (a.k.a. Lianna Empowers)

2022 Lianna Empowers

Grown Sexy Wisdom : 5 Grown Ass Ways to Create a Life that Turns You ON!

To order additional copies of this title, e-mail:
liannaempowers@gmail.com

The author may be contacted at the following e-mail address:

liannaempowers@gmail.com

First printing April 2022

Grown Sexy Wisdom : 5 Grown Ass Ways to Create a Life that Turns You ON! / VICA Publishing
ISBN: 979-8-9860001-0-7

Printed in the U S A,

# DEDICATION

To my daughters, Alexandria and Erica Gardner, you have my unconditional love always. You are my greatest gift.

To my grandson, Jace, thank you for infusing me with the joy of living and for opening my eyes to my inner child again. You are my greatest teacher. I love you to the moon and beyond!

To my sisters, Gianna, Robyn, and Tracy, as well as my brother, Wayne, thank you for the love and the laughs. I have learned so much about my own life from you all.

To my mother, Beverly, thank you for the sacrifice, strength, love and wisdom you have always shown in raising us alone. I know it wasn't easy, but you did one heck of a job! I love you dearly.

To all my beautiful friends, you know who you are!! Thank you for being there for me always. I love each and every one of you more than you'll ever know!

To my lifelong friend Walt, thank you for always listening and for being my greatest cheerleader. Without you, these words may not have come to pass.

To the Creator, thank you for the beautiful journey on which I've been led, to laugh, to cry, to learn, to grow. I am eternally grateful for life and living. I vow to live to my greatest potential.

# ACKNOWLEDGEMENTS

I am so grateful and thankful for all the people who have contributed to the creation, inspiration and success of this book. First and foremost, I want to thank the Universe for guiding me to the point of understanding what it means to align with all that is possible for me, and for inspiring me to manifest it beautifully in this lifetime!

Thank you to all of my amazing mentors and coaches that the Universe so graciously blessed me with on my journey, including David Meltzer, Julie Christopher, Master Sri Akarshana, Tjibaria Pijloo, Mary Morrissey, Ryan Eliason, Rhonda Britten, and Shereen Thor. You all have touched my life in immeasurable ways and have given me the gift of being able to see what is possible for me. Thank you for teaching me what it means to live a life of selfless service to others. I can never repay you enough for the joy you've brought to me.

To my book creation team, the amazing Nim Stant, Carrie Barnhill, and the entire crew…thank you for working your magic to bring this book, this dream to fruition for me. I could not have done any of this without your creativity, time and positive energy. I appreciate all of you!

Finally, thank you to all the *Grown Sexy Wisdom* women who inspire me to serve as I do every day! It is my life's passion to help you see the wisdom, beauty, and power that exists within every one of you. Create a life that turns you on, no fear, no excuses, no regrets. The time for your freedom is NOW. I love you!

# CONTENTS

# Chapter 5

# Chapter 6

# Chapter 7

# *Introduction*

*"If anything viewed as negative has happened on your journey thus far, turn the page, create a new chapter and write your own positive story. Then, bless humanity with the wisdom you have gained from traveling through the experience."* – **Molly Friedenfeld**

It all boils down to this, it's your life…RECLAIM IT.

For so long, you've put yourself last while putting others first. You may be:

- married
- divorced
- single
- with or without children
- career-oriented
- a stay-at-home-mom
- an entrepreneur

or one of a million other things, but you've never given yourself permission to create the life you really want for yourself.

*Now you are standing at the crossroads, wondering which way to go.*

If you've experienced anything near what I've experienced in life, putting others first may have also caused you a tremendous amount of personal pain:

- physically

- mentally
- emotionally
- spiritually

It may have also caused deep feelings of:

- resentment
- regret
- self-doubt
- shame
- lack of self-esteem
- fear
- and most of all, guilt

for even thinking about leaving behind what you don't want and choosing instead to focus on your own wants, needs, and desires. I know what it means to long to express yourself as the YOU you've evolved to yet feel trapped and unable to move forward.

When is NOW going to be the right time for you to put on your big girl panties and realize that in order for anything to change in your life, you've got to grow your ass up, once and for all, and make some decisions for YOU? It's time to accept responsibility for your life and the role you play in the creation of it, if you want to go from merely existing to *really* living.

Let's get some facts straight.

**#GrownSexyWisdom Fact #1**: *We have to die to our past selves in order to create and embrace a new way of being.*

Nothing empowers you more toward change than becoming

aware of what you've been doing to hold yourself back, and developing your 'willingness muscle' to move beyond your comfort zone. You won't ever be inspired to leave it if you're still comfortable there, so take time to focus on the uncomfortable parts.

Here is a sampling of things we often struggle with at this stage of the game:

- Are you addicted to catering to others?

If so, would *now* be a good time to let go of that way of living in order to live the grown ass life you deserve? Jobs, bosses, clergy, parents...who gets most of your attention? Oftentimes, it's our adult children we tend to cater to the most. I love my kids unconditionally, but I'm a firm believer in you have to *let them go in order to let them grow.* It took me years of enabling them to figure that one out. What changed the game for me was the following quote I read in *Change Your Thoughts–Change Your Life: Living the Wisdom of the Tao,* by self-help and spiritual author Dr. Wayne Dyer. *"Your children are not your children. They are the sons and daughters of Life's longing for itself. They come through you but not from you."* That made perfectly good sense to me. We have to allow our children to have their own journeys and experiences in life, so that they can do what their souls came here to do, without trying to control them.

- Do you have perpetual victim syndrome?

If you believe life happens *to you* rather than *for you,* you have a victim mentality. Think about it and be honest with yourself. Have you gone through life being a victim of everyone and every situation? How's that working out for you—are you feeling empowered?

- Have you allowed your circumstances and a lackful way of thinking to hold you back?

Do you think that life is a bitch because it's so hard? Have struggle and never having enough become the complete focus of your everyday life?

Sometimes, you hold onto things that allow you to make excuses for why you can't move forward, without even being aware you're doing this. Everything from your miserable job, your crappy ex-husband, friends, and relationships that don't serve your highest good. All those things are draining the life force energy from you.

Drop your attachments to anything you've given your power away to, including circumstances, material comforts, people, thoughts, even habits and beliefs. Allow yourself to let go of that baggage so you can grow. That's the only way creating the next and best chapter of your life can take place! If you're willing to take the leap, this is where you'll really take back and start to own your true power.

I'm here to put you on notice that you matter; your life MATTERS!

You may have been:

- Used
- Abused and mistreated
- Generally stuck in a rut
- Disconnected from who you really are
- Wondering at times, "What's wrong with me?"

4

First, let's get one thing straight: you've been misguided. There's nothing wrong with you, and you don't need fixing, you simply need to reconnect to your wholeness, the TRUTH of who you are at your *core. You* are a masterpiece, created for this moment and all the moments past, good, and what you call 'bad.' However, you may not have had the awareness to recognize your unique power to transform in the moment.

Here's something else you may not have known: you were born with everything you need for this journey. You already possess the power within you to grab hold of your life and create an amazing present and an unrecognizably awesome future—at any time you choose. Sometimes, you just need a little help reconnecting to your *Grown Sexy Wisdom*, your power source, from a guide who has navigated this uncharted territory and can help you gain clarity for your path forward. That guide is ME!

**GrownSexyWisdom Fact #2:** *Giving yourself permission to own your power and decide what you deserve is a game changer.*

You may remember in *The Wizard of Oz* when Dorothy realizes she's had the power all along to click the heels of her ruby red slippers together and go home to Kansas? Sis, you've had that same power in you all along! You have the power to transcend the traumas and dramas of your youth and leave behind all the childhood conditioning from your parents, neighbors, friends, and other assorted family members, naysayers and dreamkillers. The program you're running has left you not even knowing who you are. Let's get reacquainted with your truth and on the road toward becoming aware of and owning your power.

5

Maybe what you've always wanted is to BE multiple things. You may have many interests and pursuits that you're passionate about, but have never taken the time to explore them. You might even be feeling that your life is a bit incomplete at this point. Perhaps you are now finding that not allowing yourself to be what you came here to be, or do what you came here to do, has been the root cause of your deep longing for a sense of fulfillment. So, you have done nothing to advance yourself in the direction you want to go. The hamster wheel is getting a bit rusty, but it's still chugging along, with you hanging on for dear life, holding on to the same habitual thinking and way of being that keeps you stranded.

One thing I want to make very clear—and the main reason I wrote this book—is to show you that you've gained the wisdom of the ages, through all your life's experiences, all the ups and downs the ebbs and flows, all the skills you developed, your gifts and talents, the situational knowledge you've acquired, even through all the loves and all the losses. This practical wisdom combined with your divine feminine essence is your unique superpower. You inherently know what's right for you, what you like and don't like, what makes your heart sing and what doesn't. Deep down you know what you want and deserve for your life and are very clear, but you've never allowed yourself to let go so it can joyfully rise into your consciousness.

Let me make it crystal clear to you right now. Know beyond the shadow of a doubt that you have *earned the right* to live as you see fit and to create the BEST next chapter of your life on your terms. You are the director, the composer, and the narrator of your OWN life.

6

The most powerful secret sauce you have…is your *Grown Sexy Wisdom.*

Here are 5 Grown Ass Secrets to Creating a Life that Turns You ON!

# Chapter 1

---·◈·---

# What is Grown Sexy Wisdom?

*"You carry within your Divine Feminine Essence the mystical, brilliant stardust of a million light years, just waiting for you to tap into its infinite supply of light, love, prosperity, and abundance and align it with your life."*
**– Lianna Gardner**

# A Painful Reckoning

All my life, I had put others' needs before my own. In school, sports, career, child rearing, relationships, and friendships, I allowed what I came to learn was my trauma of wanting to be loved, accepted, appreciated, and acknowledged to dominate my life. This hidden hurdle was deeply tied to being part of a broken family as well as having certain school-age experiences. It led to an overwhelming fear of rejection and a people-pleasing personality that resulted in a whole lot of internal pain and heartache.

Things were a bit complicated because I had a knowing deep down that I was extremely gifted and talented in so many areas, capable of being way more than I ever allowed myself to be. I just didn't have the confidence or the self-esteem to surmount the issues that were blocking me from *becoming*. As it turned out, it took my journey of finding the courage to leave an abusive marriage to awaken me to my inner power and start to grow my spiritual muscle. I had to understand my connection to myself. The Divine seed had been planted, but it took years for it to fully bloom. It was the internal voice of God, the power I had within, that led me to understand that I could not become the woman I was meant to be within the context of my marriage. I gratefully grew the inner strength by tapping into this Divine power to escape my marriage. I became a divorced, single mother with two amazing little girls, 2 and 4 at the time, on an 'us against the world' mission. All I wanted was to create a happy, healthy life and home for my babies. Putting my children's needs first was a no-brainer for me as a conscientious, deeply devoted mother who loved her two daughters and was hell-bent on making sure they grew into happy and successful human beings.

During this time, my girls and I became like the 3 Musketeers...*All for One and One for All*...me taking them on vacations, hosting family gatherings, providing for their every need, and doing my best to be the rational, level-headed Mom I thought served my girls' needs best. We ate together, played together, and enjoyed life together. Dedicated Mom that I was, I fought tooth and nail for them during their school years. If I thought something was off kilter with their education...I simply wanted to do my best to help them have as normal a childhood as possible in the absence of their father.

Raising my two daughters as a single parent was a challenge in and of itself. I got a bigger taste of what it meant to be both parents to them, as the full-time responsibility was all mine, with the exception of every other weekend. There were also goals and dreams I had held deep in my heart that I longed to pursue, but at the same time, I knew putting my beauties first was my commitment to them until such time I felt it feasible to focus on myself. I also chose to forgo dating on the weekends I had them, which made relationships challenging. But, I didn't want to introduce them to anyone I felt I wasn't going to be with long term, because I didn't want them to get attached to that person and have men coming in and out of their lives. That would have hurt them emotionally, I reasoned. So, I was very lonely at times.

The time, love and attention I put into them over time, however, didn't prove to be enough for their growth and well-being. There were a host of other mitigating factors that played into the grand scheme of things. One such factor was having a controlling, self centered father, who had been abusive to me during our marriage. He had never fully shared in my daughters' rites of passage, or validation of them as young women. This led to one daughter having an unhealthy obsession with finding love and acceptance in teenage boys who were up to no good, and the other wanting me to continually coddle her and cater to her every need. I wanted desperately to find someone I could share a relationship with, who would bring balance to all of our lives, and who could show them what a healthy relationship between two people who loved each other looked like. Unfortunately, that did not happen while I was raising them. All of this led to trouble in paradise and a cascading turn of events during their turbulent teens that blindsided and hurt me to the core.

I recall vividly the moment when my standing as a parent, and my core wisdom, first came under attack—it was truly a 'mind blown' smack in the face for me. This came at a time when I had been trying to provide life guidance to my youngest teenage daughter and my niece, whom I'd taken under my wing, on their paths to adulthood. These two had formed an unhealthy alliance and joined forces against me, based on things they didn't like about my choices. They were on a rampage about my life as it related to theirs, especially with regard to things they thought I should and shouldn't do. Mind you, they hated my new boyfriend, my free-spirited lifestyle, my choices, everything that didn't coincide with their vision of how they thought I should live and do things. It was purely selfish, especially as it related to them and what they felt I *should* be doing for them. These two, along with my eldest daughter, seriously thought they had all the answers to my life and theirs and that their answers to these mysteries far outweighed and outclassed mine. For example, they felt that since they didn't ask to be born, that I as a parent was supposed to be there for them and provide for their *every* need through infinity. Another example was their insistence that the man I was dating wasn't right for me, and that I didn't need him in my life because they didn't like the fact that he helped me with things that, up until that point, I had done myself. They literally said to me, "We don't want your wisdom…it's old school, and we're new school; yours is so outdated."

Armaggedon be damned, this was the end of the world as I knew it. I was furious. This personal attack on my parenting, and all I'd learned and drawn upon in my life to not only guide and raise them, but self-guide my own life, became a source of resentment between us for a very long time. How dare they minimize all that I'd been through. They cast aside so callously the lessons I'd learned across a lifetime as if they had no meaning. *All* that I'd done to this point was to put them *first* their entire lives, out of sheer, unconditional love for them. I thought, "You haven't been through or experienced the things that have ***earned me the right*** to be able to share these valuable lessons with you." All I wanted was to provide loving guidance for them on their life's journey. During that time when they started to assert their young womanhood, the three of them rejected any wisdom I sought to share with them. They, like so many other kids of their generation, believed they always knew better about what was best for themselves, for me, and all the other adults in their lives.

Their resentment toward me was due to the fact that I had been starting to assert and allow myself to actually have and express some of my own needs and to ease away in baby steps from the 99% of things I still did for them. I remember when my youngest daughter Erica and I had our first run-in about me making her older sister, Alexandria, drive her to and from basketball practice, versus me doing it myself. "Why are you making Alex drive me to practice? You used to drive me all the time," she complained.

I couldn't believe she was being that selfish. "But I've been doing everything for you guys by myself for 16 years!! I made her get her driver's license, that she didn't even want to get, because I'm worn out. I need some help!" I explained.

Erica swore I was superwoman. She has told me since that having others step in and do things to help me ruined her image of me, because she felt my strength was in doing everything for the two of them, on my own. When I fell off that pedestal, it seriously destroyed my credibility with her, and there was no turning back. Then there was also the issue of me having a boyfriend. No matter what I did to try to integrate us together as a family , she wasn't having it, because he broke up the nucleus. Erica wanted me all to herself. Talk about stressful, I had deprived myself of any love interest the entire time they were growing up. I needed this relationship with a man I felt safe with, at this particular time in my life. I sincerely thought they had grown mature enough to learn to handle a little more responsibility, make some of their own decisions, and become a little more independent from Mama as they approached their final years of high school.

Boy, was I wrong.

Although motherhood, especially single motherhood, was a very beautiful experience and something I took deeply personally, it was also one of the most stressful, traumatic and painful things I've ever experienced in my life.

During this painful reckoning, I knew that in order to survive, I needed to retreat within, reevaluate my inner landscape, reconnect to my truth and find the strength to stand in my power. I had never been challenged like this before by my own flesh and blood.

It was this place of pain, along with a series of life lessons over the next several years, that led me on a journey of discovery to find out who I was and what I was really made of. I learned what it meant to evolve and grow and become keenly aware of my inner self and its relation to my life. This is where the *Grown Sexy Wisdom* revolution was born!

## <u>You've Earned the Right</u>

Even though your beautiful, amazing soul has spent a lifetime putting other people and their needs first, while often stifling your own needs, wants and desires, at this stage of the game, you're ready to create the next and best chapter of your life so you can go out of here with a bang, not a damn whimper.

I was divorced, had two teenage daughters with one foot out the door, had lovingly played the role of mommy and daddy as well as big sister, bad sister to my siblings, had been the abused wife, overly dedicated employee and general Mrs. Nice Guy to everyone in my life. But I felt like a people-pleasing victim. Even in the midst of my perceived victimhood, life was always calling me to be bigger and greater, it was calling me to serve...to do more and to be more and express the innermost machinations of my heart. So, in taking stock of all that I was and what I wanted to be, I found what drove me and what was calling me forth.

What turns you ON, what lights you UP? Do you even know anymore? Do you have the courage, commitment, and drive to stretch yourself, to grow, expand, and ascend? If you aren't doing any of those things, you need to start hanging out with people who raise your light to another level so you can get where you want to go.

Have you ever taken time out to sit with your desires, those passions that are calling you forward, and identify them? Do you know what they are? Or is it sometimes you think you know what they are, but you've never given yourself permission to go there? There's something unique at the core of who you are that is your truth, the you that you were destined to be from the day you were born. Your truth always seeks ways to express itself, even if you try to tamp the fire down with fears, limiting beliefs, thoughts, habits, and negative attitudes.

When you keep your passions and your dreams alive, that's what gives you *LIFE* and keeps every cell in your being vibrant and healthy. Giving up your dream represents a death within you…a part of your soul that dies because you aren't giving it life, or allowing yourself to experience that joy. If you've ever searched for happiness but had trouble finding it…9 times out of 10 it's because you've never allowed yourself to have what makes you happy or go where life is calling you.

Have you ever seen the 80s blockbuster movie *Flashdance,* starring Jennifer Beals, my favorite *'take your passion and make it happen'* inspirational movie of all time? That empowering flick sparked a flame in me that carries through to this day. It was a love story between a man and a woman, but it was also a self-love story, with many lessons around how to believe in yourself and to be persistent in going after your dreams no matter what obstacles you may face.

16

Any time I was ever up against a life challenge that seemed insurmountable, I reached for Irene Cara's version of the title song, *"Flashdance...What a Feeling."* I would crank the volume on that sucker, close my eyes and lose myself in it. By the time the song was over, I was bouncing around like Rocky (another inspiring movie) at the top of the stairs in Philadelphia, waving my fists in the air and shouting 'YES!!!' at the top of my lungs, feeling like I was invincible! It is truly magical when you make the pictures of your dreams come alive in your mind by creating a vision, and in your heart by igniting the flame of your passion. Put the vision and passion together with the ACTION necessary to allow the Universe to do its thing, and it will conspire to help you bring your vision to life! Then, you've got a recipe for reconnecting to your CORE, the truth of who you are, which is your birthright!

Think about it...you've been laying the groundwork your entire life for THIS moment. You've paid your dues. The love, the joy, the sorrow, the pain, hard lessons and heartaches, promotions and demotions. Your unique body of work consists of an endless sea of life lessons you can readily draw upon to figure out how to look your circumstances in the eye and determine your path forward, despite the challenges you may face.

*GrownSexyWisdom* is about mastering the art of living your authentic essence.

**Practical You**     **Divine Feminine**

= *Grown Sexy Wisdom*

It is the culmination of your *practical* self:

- All the wisdom that you've derived from life's lessons
- The situational knowledge you've gained
- Your gifts, talents, passions and creativity
- The skills you've learned and the experience you've attained
- Who you are in the present, and who you are evolving into

*Plus* your *Divine Feminine* Self

I like to describe the Divine Feminine as your *Goddess* self. It is you fully realizing the sacred essence and truth of who you are. The beautiful, intuitive, heart centered energy of you standing fully in your power and nurturing yourself in order to create a more harmonious world, inside and out.

18

It's important to understand that Divine Feminine and Divine Masculine Energy exist in *all* things; however, it is clear that having to live in a male-dominated world, where masculine qualities and pursuits are king, we lose balance between the two energies. When we become aware of this and give ourselves the self-care we need to restore this balance and begin to reconnect to our hearts and create from that space, we come into the full realization of our power.

Meld the *practical* together with the *Divine,* and this is your inner superpower, the authentic essence of all that you are. Top it off with your smoldering self-confidence, air of invincibility, and your authentic aura, and you get a whole lot of *sexy* oozing from the middle. This grand sum of *Grown Sexy Wisdom* forms the unique foundation of *you.*

You've fought like hell in life's trenches to get to this stage. It is everything badass about you that makes you irresistibly you and can elevate your life to the next level—your greatest chapter, if you allow it.

Why settle for riding the rest of your life out in your comfort zone when you've still got so much to give? It's time to create a life that turns you ON!

So, I'm putting you on notice. Throw 'average' living out the window. You've got work to do to stretch even higher toward your Divinely gifted potential. Ask yourself…how can I serve? Stop letting your dreams collect dust sitting on the shelf. It's time to realign with and revive them! If you've birthed new goals and dreams that you've dared not pursue simply because you aren't sure how to get them out of your mind and into your reality, now is the time to bring them to life. Don't become a statistic, stuck on the sidelines letting life pass you by. Sing your song, dance your dance, don't die with your music inside!

The whole of who you are, the you you've evolved to, has *earned the right* to express yourself in any way you feel that you are being called forth. You have the right to tap into and share your *Grown Sexy Wisdom* with the rest of the world, in order to expand, ascend, and live life on your terms. Now that's creating a life that *turns you ON* and will allow you to light up the world!!

## Letting Go of What No Longer Serves You

Now that you know that *Grown Sexy Wisdom* is the awesome AF internal *GrownSexyPower* you possess, you might wonder why, even though you have this treasure chest full of personal magic that will allow you to create a life beyond your wildest dreams, you haven't arrived yet. Why can't you figure out exactly what direction you'd like to go? What is holding you back?

For me, it was:

- Fear of making a decision
- Lack of clarity for what I really wanted
- Low self-esteem
- Lack of confidence
- Worry about what others thought about me
- Not trusting myself enough
- Fear of leaving my paycheck behind for the 'unknown'
- Bright shiny object syndrome
- Overwhelm
- Self-victimization

- Using others as an excuse for why I couldn't move forward
- Fear of success
- Self-sabotage
- Fear of going it alone

Shall I go on? Is your list of hurdles as lengthy as mine? What does your list look like? Dig deep and jot down what keeps you from shifting into a life you love at this *'you first'* stage in your life:

_____

_____

_____

_____

_____

Now, delve just a little deeper into the vast recesses of your beautiful mind. Did you hit on everything...or is there something there that your ego won't allow you to admit? Write it here:

_____

_____

_____

_____

_____

Did anything surprise you? Did anything new come up for you?

Sometimes it takes time to get to the heart of what keeps you from moving forward. It could be a trauma, a belief, thought, habit, or attitude that you've held onto for years. But don't sweat it, I just unearthed a trauma that had evolved into a belief that had kept me trapped much of my entire adult life!

While it took me a lifetime to bring it to the surface so I could heal it, I'm telling you without a doubt, it is so worth it to finally be able to recognize and release that particular trauma so it no longer controls my life.

I'm of the mindset that even if you haven't entirely gotten to the heart of all your limiting beliefs (beliefs that hold you back from your true potential), this doesn't have to hold you back from creating a vision and shooting for the stars. Do it afraid, and do it before you're ready. That's some bold warrior woman shit! If you are on the road toward your goal or dream and doing the work, at the very least you're showing the Universe that you are willing to take action no matter what, so that it can move for you in ways that will allow you to manifest what you desire. In order to let go of the things that hold you back, you've got to learn to let go of ego and get brutally honest with yourself. It's called doing the shadow work.

Shadow work involves getting in touch with those parts of you that you've repressed. In other words, your, dare I say it…dark side. Whew, this is a process few like to venture into, due to not wanting those memories and any associated pain to resurface. Also, there can be a lot of shame, embarrassment, and guilt associated with things that have happened in your past. If you want to take this journey, you've got to let it rise to the top so you can confront and begin to heal it in order to move on from it.

Each of us is made up of light and darkness. The journey to self-love means that you learn to love and accept yourself for all of who you are and learn to live with and love the multiple layers of you that make up your amazing whole. When you love yourself, and love others as yourself, you are emitting the highest light frequency. What greater good can we do for humanity! In this state of being, it is easiest to keep your dark side at bay. Knowing and understanding that you are both darkness and light shines an entirely different perspective on life.

Love every layer that is you!

Anytime the darkness feels like it is taking over your light, take a break and remove yourself from the chaos. Go to your favorite quiet place, your bathtub, hot tub, your bedroom, nature… light some incense or a nice aromatic candle and turn on some high vibrational music, or simply tune into the wind on your face and the sun on your head and just breathe. One of my favorite music retreats is the Pandora Zen Music Garden Station. No words, just soothing melodies and relaxing tunes. This is one of my go-to processes which, without fail, helps me calm down, slow down, breathe, and recenter my energy. All of these things help with concentrating, focusing, and sleeping…the perfect tools for rebalancing your energies.

Here are a few other ways you can rebalance yourself:

- **Exercise**. Yes, ladies…get moving! Exercise is a form of meditation. It revitalizes your body-mind-spirit, boosting your oxygen levels, and allows your body to use its energy more efficiently. It's better than anything out there for making you feel amazing!
- **Meditate**. Quieting the mind and focusing on your breathing helps calm you down and also reduces stress. Meditating also helps us cultivate our inner landscape, connecting us more to our core source of power, which leads to spiritual growth and connectedness.

- **Drink Water.** Water helps your body flush out toxins, which are detrimental to your physical, mental, emotional, and spiritual health.
- **Eat Clean Foods.** Foods have a vibration as well. Organic foods help your body feel better since you are eating foods without pesticides and other toxic additives. Have you ever felt bad after eating? Does your diet consist of preserved foods with inorganic additives that make you feel like crap? Try substituting those inorganic and processed foods with organic foods for a week or two and see how much better your body feels.

Letting go of what does not serve you is a process that involves getting in tune with your body-mind-spirit and releasing anything that is clogging up your energy and doesn't allow it to flow easily. When you let go of old thoughts, beliefs, habits, and attitudes that have held you bound, then you can truly flow with the positive and high vibrational energy of life. This leads to feelings of happiness, love, and joy as well as the manifestation of what you desire.

The bottom line here is…are you a badass or is your life bass-ackwards? Living your *Grown Sexy Wisdom* life involves being willing to own your inner power and do the work necessary to elevate your life to the next level. It's getting down to the nitty gritty that exists within you! Dive in and do what's necessary to move out the old. Allow yourself to breathe in and embody all that is good, mighty, and powerful within you! Discover the raw and beautiful essence of who you are. Remember, the best thing about this is that, contrary to popular belief, you aren't 'broken' and you don't need fixing. You simply need to reconnect to your CORE, the truth of who you are. That's what becoming aware of and embracing your *Grown Sexy Wisdom* will allow you to do.

24

Living your truth is your birthright. You can only open your mind to new possibilities and opportunities for your life if you know and understand that you were gifted with everything you need for this journey from the day you were born. It's time to tap into it and step into the fullness of your being!

## Autumn…Allowing Growth and Ascension

One of the most beautiful transformations and examples of *Grown Sexy Wisdom* living that I've ever had the privilege to witness was by a very dear friend of mine by the name of Autumn.

Autumn was a hairdresser in the town that I moved to after my divorce in 2000. She was the only African American stylist that I knew of within 30 miles of my home, so I called and made an appointment for her to cut my hair one weekend.

Wow, did we hit it off. She gave my self-esteem such a huge boost, raving about how beautiful I was and how she admired me as a person. I needed that blast of positivity and self-confidence so badly. Plus, I needed a really good friend. We found that we had so much in common and were dealing with similar issues in our lives. Abusive marriages, low self-esteem, lack of confidence, uncomfortable with shining in our beauty. As I look back on it, she was my mirror...when I looked at her, I saw me. She was sassy, with a hilarious sense of humor, vulnerable, super friendly and genuinely down to earth, with an aura as bright as the sun. On top of all that, she was one of the most beautiful and authentic people I'd ever met.

Something about her struck me as strange, though. She was

an introvert who kept to herself quite a bit, rarely letting anyone else in and always wore black from head to toe, constantly covering up her long hair with a skull cap. She seemed to never allow herself to break free of that persona. I found it rather odd, especially since she was drop dead gorgeous. But as we grew closer, I discovered why she kept herself hidden in plain sight.

Autumn had a rather tumultuous upbringing...suffering heartbreaking ridicule from a close family member who made fun of the size of her bosom as she was growing up. Ladies, you know what that does to a young girl's body image. It was this ridicule added with the lack of a father presence and more emotional, mental, and psychological abuse she'd suffered in her family that led her to cover herself in shame and retreat inward, afraid to let go and allow her inner and outer beauty to flow.

Her adult life played out in trauma after trauma as well. When I met her, she was married to an ex-pro football player who was not only abusive, she found out he was cheating on her. I remember going over to their house one day...she'd called me over just wanting some company and a friendly listening ear after some drama with her husband the night before. I wanted to be her go-to friend, because I knew she needed someone to confide in and lean on, and I definitely needed a close friend/sister relationship as I had left my hometown for this new place after my divorce.

Soon after she discovered his infidelity, she decided that now was the time to file for divorce, leave this baller and step out on her own. She knew she deserved better but wasn't quite at the place yet where her self-esteem or confidence would allow her to connect with anyone right away. She needed some 'me' time.

During this time, our sisterhood grew stronger. I enjoyed sharing time and energy with her any chance I got—it gave me the laughter and life I needed, and an alternative to being a full-time mom.

A couple of years later, she grew the courage to start dating again. OMG did we have a blast talking about the guys we would date online…she had me laughing till my sides split and she was dry heaving (a common side effect of our hilarious talks together). She met a guy named 'Anthony' who lived in the Dayton area of Ohio where he was employed by the military.

The beginning of that relationship was a heart-wrenching rollercoaster…emotions up and down and all around. I remember our deep discussions about what his motives were with his first wife, and whether or not his kids were controlling his life, and so much more. She shared with me that he was a poet and that he loved reading at spoken word events. Those two shared in many wonderful things he liked to do, even though she wanted to push him away and sabotage the relationship because she wasn't sure she could trust him yet. But she discovered after several months of dating that she'd found herself a keeper.

During this time, while Autumn was dating Anthony, I introduced her to my oldest sister, G, who visited frequently. The three of us soon became great buddies, with my sister joining our 'sisterhood.' G and I realized that this was the perfect opportunity to help transform this beautiful woman and all that amazing light we saw within her, helping her embrace that light so she could shine brighter than she ever had—so we set out to do just that.

We had the greatest time ever, going shopping together and picking out things for Autumn that we knew she would never try on or buy if left to her own devices. Anytime we went out, we always made it a rule that Autumn was not allowed to pick out or try on anything that was dark-colored; that way, we could get her to see how amazing she looked in colors and in different styles. I could see that Autumn was really enjoying this time in her life. Finally, she gave in and allowed the transformation…and she absolutely loved it!

This woman glowed in her new glamourous brightly colored dresses, tops, and slacks. We had a great time picking out purses and jewelry together, and I kid you not, a star was born!

With her newfound confidence, she began to shed the darkness in her life and embraced the sassy, sexy confidence she oozed. That was when her relationship with Anthony went to a whole different and life-changing level. One day she came to me with some news that I thought would destroy my life. She told me that Anthony was being transferred to a Naval Base outside of Atlanta, GA and that she was considering moving there to be with him. I was so happy for her, but was devastated at the same time, because my best friend could be leaving me.

He moved and, sure enough, a few months later, she made the decision that he was who she wanted to be with and that she'd be leaving town for good. Believe me when I say I was heartbroken. My old fear of rejection raised its ugly head, and instead of us having a good sendaway, it was a tear-ridden, chaotic day when she came to say goodbye. We ended up in a huge argument because I was so hurt that she was leaving. She never wanted to talk about the move or my feelings surrounding it. Hence, I was forced to suppress those emotions, which was extremely painful. I felt like there was no closure for me. So I watched her drive off, and that was the last I saw of her for several months, until we forgave each other for the goodbye argument and started talking to one another again.

While she was in Georgia, Autumn basked in her newfound freedom to be the beautiful woman inside and out that she'd evolved into. She felt bolstered by the deep love and admiration of a man who loved her unconditionally, which allowed her to learn how to love and be loved again. She blossomed even further into something unrecognizably beautiful. Autumn and Anthony were soon married. As a result, she broke further out of her shell, making new and amazing friends, repairing familial relationships, and always paying what my sister and I had given her forward. The light within her grew ever brighter as she never shied away from giving to others just for the sake of giving. I loved watching her step out of her comfort zone and lean in to doing things her husband suggested they do, just for the fun of it—things she'd always resisted before. Together, they were a force to be reckoned with and were the most beautiful example of how a man and a woman can build, renew, and love each other I'd ever witnessed in my entire life.

On Valentine's Day, 2014, which was their 5-year wedding anniversary, Autumn's world came crashing down. Her wonderful husband was away at a rehab center several miles away, recuperating from knee replacement surgery a few weeks before, and she received a phone call that devastated her beyond repair. Anthony had passed away from a blood clot that had traveled to his lung, a risk of the knee surgery he'd had.

She called me, and I was so blown away, I couldn't believe it. In fact, I was speechless. I didn't know what to say. Autumn was inconsolable and, quite honestly, I wasn't sure she'd survive this. For once in her life, she had everything she ever wanted, and they'd just started really building a life together. But just like that, he was gone.

The pain of that day was something she could not shake loose. She suffered from deep depression, was suicidal at times, and I was really concerned about her. But she had an amazing support system—me, my sister, the other awesome friends she'd made in Georgia—and it was leaning on that system that helped her survive and get through it as best she could.

About 3 years later, she began dating because she knew Anthony would never want to see her alone or deny herself the opportunity to love again. Soon we found ourselves laughing and shooting the breeze about her dating escapades, and I truly enjoyed reconnecting with my sister.

The next year brought more devastating news, when Autumn told me she had a benign brain tumor and that she was going through with surgery to remove it. We discussed it at length, but she was determined to get it out of her body, because it was causing headaches and pain that she didn't want to deal with.

After the surgery, she initially wasn't the same. She'd suffered a stroke and had to learn to walk and talk again. Believe me when I say this woman had 9 lives because she had been through the ringer and back, but through it all kept laughing, smiling…even while inside she was dying at times. She never fully recovered from the surgery and the stroke, suffering a lot of pain and side effects after, but that never allowed her beauty, her spirit, or her generous, humorous nature to skip a beat. She remained committed to expanding, elevating, and ascending in life, because that's who she was. A beautiful soul on a mission to live her amazing light.

On Labor Day, September 6, 2021, Autumn, my beautiful friend and sister, unexpectedly passed away. I was completely devastated. Here was this spunky, hilarious, gorgeous, generous sister gone, just like that. The family chose not to do an autopsy, leaving all of us to wonder what caused her untimely death.

I'm still getting over it and many days find myself in tears surrounding this loss—but the most amazing thing about my dear friend and sister is that she learned to live in the present and to love out loud. She allowed herself to leave her comfort zone in the prime of her life, despite her past insecurities, traumas and beliefs, and surrender to love, with faith that the unknown would be OK. She learned to live in the present each day, opening herself to living and becoming all that she never allowed herself to be in her previous way of being. She had arrived at her Turning Point and made a choice that changed her life forever.

Tomorrow is not promised. Approach each day you are gifted

with excitement, joy and love.

Allow yourself, like Autumn, to let go of the comfortable pain of your past, and decide to live in the present, with all its endless possibilities! You will blossom into a way of being beyond your wildest imagination. Give yourself permission to try new things, to open your heart to giving and receiving love, and to adventure to new places. Love out loud, and let your soul expand and fill your container with joy!

Open yourself to fully accessing your inner power...your *Grown Sexy Wisdom*, tapping into the essence of all that you are and allow it to guide you. You'll find that you have everything you need for creating the experiences of a lifetime. Your best is yet to come. Life, love, happiness, and adventure await!

# Chapter 2

## *GrownSexySecret # 1:* How to Navigate Your Turning Point...How the Hell Did I Get HERE?

Life comes at us daily. It truly is our thoughts, habits, beliefs, attitudes, emotions, level of courage, and perception of ourselves that determine how we will navigate our circumstances and decide where we will go from here.

A Turning Point is a moment in time when you are standing at a crossroads and making a decision that will impact your present and your future, one that causes you to shift your priorities. Right now, after all you've given in your personal blood, sweat and tears to get others across the finish line, you get to decide how you will blaze your own trail from this point forward. What lights you up and makes your heart sing? What will be your legacy? What mark will you leave upon the world?

Lord, were these turning points a freaking scary place for me. I had so much I wanted to do, but so many fears and 'what if's' surrounding all of it! Turning points like being tied by the heartstrings to my teenage daughters, yet feeling the Divine pull of my own heart wanting to expand and impact lives on such a greater level—that part of me was dying to be expressed. But, what did I want to do? What choices could I make for myself? Another Turning Point was when I was in an abusive job situation that was literally killing me, wondering what could I do to leave that? My body-mind-spirit was severely suffering, but like many of you, I was tied to the paycheck and financial remuneration for my family's sake. I made the decision to stay in my 'comfortable pain,' and it continued to cost me dearly.

Do you feel me? How often do we stay in the comfortable

pain of our comfort zones, putting up with things that eat away at our self-esteem and our happiness? Based upon my unique experiences, my life had evolved to a place where I wanted to express myself in a deeply profound way, empowering others who had been stuck on the sidelines watching life pass them by. I had been stuck much of my life, all because I was afraid to go where I was being called to go.

I remember many nights lying in bed anxiously reflecting on my life and the dreams I'd had as a little girl, wondering where they all went; why did I allow them to die? It's funny, as shy and insecure as I was, I actually wanted to be a famous singer when I grew up. I loved to sing and had an Olivia Newton John, Barbara Streisand kind of voice…able to light up the stratosphere with my soprano notes. My vocal coach even told me I should have been an opera singer LOL! Despite the fact that I was scared absolutely shitless of singing in public, I found a way to do it anyway, despite my fears. This is an example of a Turning Point, where I made a choice that allowed me to pursue my passion.

Soon after I graduated from college, my favorite cousin connected me with her ex-boyfriend, Darryl, who had been a bass player for none other than the great Patti LaBelle. He had a small recording studio in downtown Columbus, Ohio where he produced some local groups and also had serious connections with a lot of big players in the R&B recording industry. OMG…I found my heaven on earth!

I began to practically live at the studio, sitting in on many of his sessions with local artists, and listened excitedly as Darryl chatted it up with artists like Bernadette Cooper of Klymaxx fame. Soon, my day had arrived! Late one night as Darryl and I were shooting the breeze about singing, and songs, melodies and notes, he prodded me to step up to the mic and sing solo vocals for a tune he had written. My heart began to pound out of my chest! I skittishly agreed—scared to death, but deciding this was my moment to step out of my comfort zone once and for all. It was just me and him in that dimly lit studio, the lights of all the mixing equipment lit up like a Christmas tree, and OMG was I afraid! I think it was really the fear of the rest of the world potentially hearing and judging my voice—the vulnerability I felt in the moment. *What if they don't like me?*

Talk about powerful, life changing experiences! When you are in the midst of doing something you've always dreamed about, something magical happens! It's as if heaven and earth move to create that moment and suspend it in time, holding a place for you to put your Divine spin and signature on the gift or talent you are expressing—that's sheer ecstasy. When it was over and we played back the recording, I couldn't believe it…that was me???!!!

Darryl was ecstatic…and started boasting to others about the work I'd done. He even called up Bernadette again and played it for her. She loved it! *I did it*! I actually conquered one of my greatest fears and did what I didn't think I could or would ever do! I hung with him for a couple of years and had an absolute blast singing background vocals for several local groups and jazz artists, as well as becoming a producer and talent developer for his studio. I was having the time of my life!

Soon, though, I met a man who would change my life in so many ways, and I allowed my singing dream to fade away. During this Turning Point, I chose to spend much of my time with this man who would become my future husband, cultivating our relationship and putting aside my own individual wants and needs to see where this new love interest would lead me. After all, my profound need for love, acceptance, acknowledgement, and attention, on a personal level, far outweighed my dream. What better way to feel complete than by becoming romantically involved with someone with whom I was drawn to and loved spending my time with?

This is where we *lose ourselves*. Many times, we end up making the nice, safe choice that has been ingrained in our psyche from the day we are born. Women are supposed to settle down with a nice boy, create a family, and live the American dream. We leave behind our own goals, dreams, and desires to conform to someone else's idea of how we should live our lives. We drop our dreams for our husband's dream. When the kids are born, we continue to ignore our passions in order to put them first. The killer part is when the kids grow up and move out, we realize we've never pursued any of our own dreams.

Looking back through my *Grown Sexy Wisdom* eyes, while some of my Turning Points turned out great and some not so great, I know I've gotta give myself tons of credit! I have fought through fear my entire life and done some amazing things, and I know without a doubt that you have too! However, I've also had times when my fear overpowered me, and I've pushed aside my deepest passions by failing in that moment to choose the things that would satisfy my soul.

How have you navigated the **Turning Points** in your life?

_____

_____

_____

_____

_____

How will you navigate this one differently?

_____

_____

_____

_____

_____

After all, time is marching on, and it's at a premium. I felt like I wasted so much time in my life wading around in fear.

You don't just have one or two Turning Points, you have tons of them. Depending on the *choices* you make in *this* moment, you could find yourself years later gazing up from your trance, looking around at where you are, and wondering, *How the hell did I get here?* This moment in time becomes another Turning Point in your life. *What* is the right decision for me, based on *where my life has evolved to and who I am* NOW? *Where* on earth do I want to go, and *how* do I get there?

In order to navigate the Turning Point you have arrived at right now and make choices and decisions that are in alignment with your heart, here are some *Grown Sexy Wisdom* strategies to help guide you!

1.) **Reconnect to your inner child**

You came into this world as a joyful, bouncy baby, without

38

any fears except of falling and of loud noises. You were ready to learn, grow and become based on your heart wisdom, but something happened in between birth and your destiny. Soon after you graced the earth with your presence, everyone in your life, notably your parents, family, friends, teachers, caregivers, clergy, the media, and more, started to program you according to their fears, thoughts, beliefs, habits and attitudes. So, although you were born with boundless joy in your tiny being and with everything you needed for this journey such as your gifts, talents, purpose, and Divine inner power, you began to forget this sacred knowing and have spent most of your life trying to remember and reconnect to it.

As your unique computer chip acquired its data based on everything going on around you and your interpretation of it, you continued to play and have fun, like most kids do, oblivious to the program that was beginning to insert itself into your subconscious.

But man, did we have such FUN back then!! Those were the days when you didn't have a care in the world. You could play with your friends and siblings all day, fully connected to your creativity that came to life through your vivid imagination! Back then, you played, created and dreamed about what you wanted to be when you grew up and didn't have to do much else but have fun all day, every day.

What did you dream of becoming?

_____

_____

_____

_____

_____

What made you happy and gave you the greatest joy?

_____

_____

_____

_____

_____

What types of things did you create back then that fed your heart? _(i.e., I created little side hustles that allowed me to fund my needs as a child. I also built things with my hands that were very creative and fun)_

_____

_____

_____

_____

_____

There are a couple of surefire ways you can reconnect to your inner child. One way is by quieting your mind and recalling the fun things you did, the dreams you had and the activities that made you happy. Who did you have fun with? What did you do? How can you take that joy that you were connected to then and transform it to the energy of love, joy, happiness, and freedom you want now in your life?

The second way to reconnect to your inner child is to actually _DO_ some of the things that you enjoyed doing as a child. _Do it, I dare you..._jump up and down on the bed with your grandkids, or by yourself. I swear, I've done it and laughed till I cried!! Go to a carnival and ride the rides, explore a museum, build a snow fort, have a snowball or pillow fight… talk about transmuting the energy of unknowing and indecision into a high vibing and creative flow!! You won't know what hit you when all the ideas start to come through!

40

Listen to that Divine chatter, tune into it and watch your world start to change! Forget all the old programming, it's time to pull out that old wiring and replace it with new and powerful wiring—full of brand new possibilities and opportunities!

## 2.) **Recognize the power of your story**

What is your unique STORY and how has it shaped you? Is the story you tell about yourself empowering or is it disempowering? Does it keep you stuck or has your story allowed you to soar? Think of the power your personal narrative has over you. Is it yours or someone else's?

Reflect on what you tell others about your life. In your conversations with friends or when forging relationships with others, how does your story go? Is it ego driven with a parade of masks you wear to impress others, or is it filled with talk of how you've been a victim of rotten employers, dysfunctional parents, and selfish significant others?

Your story is a powerful set of:

- thoughts
- habits
- beliefs
- attitudes
- and all the affiliated emotions, traumas, and dramas

that form your view of yourself and of life. It's a system of living you adopt for yourself that is deeply entrenched in:

- what you learned in your environment, past and present

- what you've observed and heard and how you've interpreted it
- and how you've applied this to your daily life

The more you tell it, the more it becomes a part of your core beliefs and shapes the way you interact with your world. But here's the kicker, because we live in a Universe where the law of attraction reigns supreme: you've got to recognize that the energy you put out will always equal the energy you get back. The words you think, speak, and act upon create everything in your life! What you are speaking you are giving life to!!!

Stop it!!

You are the one who creates your circumstances, you are the one who creates your problems, but you are also the one who creates the good that happens in your life. As humans, we go through positive and negative thoughts daily, but the key is not to let the negative gain momentum.

If you have a disempowering story full of fear, sorrow, complaining, grieving, self-victimization, or hanging onto the past, you're going to get more of that. Would you like a side of fries with that disempowering story?

The only way to move forward and to change the narrative is by being willing to let go of ego and begin to rewrite your story in a manner that will help you create positive shifts in your life, so you can write your next greatest chapter!

I tell you, it has taken me so long to get to this place of peace, allowing, and abundance in my life. What held me back was the story I told to myself and others about my victimhood in an abusive marriage, how I had to raise two daughters on my own, how my parents divorced when I was 9 and I never felt accepted and loved, how my first boss sexually harassed me…and on and on.

If you really want to embrace the essence of your *Grown Sexy Wisdom*, learn from your missteps. Learn to create a new and empowering story for yourself every day, simply by doing the work to shift the way you view yourself and the words you think and say about yourself.

Become more aware of what you are creating and giving life to with the power of your words. Knowing this will have a profound effect on transforming old habits that no longer serve you.

Other ways you can change the power of your story: (after each one, jot down a couple of ways you can do this)

- **Change Your Self-Talk.** Reframe your thoughts. For example, if you tell yourself that you don't have enough 'life experience' to bring to a job or other opportunity, you could change it by saying to yourself, "I'm a quick learner with the ability to adapt to any situation." Retrain your brain to focus on what you can do vs. everything you think you can't.

_____

_____

_____

_____

_____

- **Journal.** When you write about the events of your day, your feelings, your triumphs and setbacks, do it honestly and openly. Reading it back to yourself, you'll begin to see patterns where you can shift from disempowering thoughts and language to more empowering ones.

_____

_____

_____

_____

_____

- **Fortify Yourself.** Find some of your favorite affirmations. Write them down, read or repeat them daily. Or, create a 'personal disclaimer' for your life and affirm it for 5 minutes in the morning before you start your day, and 5 minutes in the evening before you go to bed.

_____

_____

_____

_____

_____

A *personal disclaimer* is something like this...

*"The thoughts and views expressed to me by others daily DO NOT represent 'my truth.' They are merely an opinion based on their perspective. In the express interest of my personal growth, I choose not to take personally the opinions of others and seek to establish my own truth."*

If you want to move forward into creating a life that turns you on, it's all about shifting your perspective. Once you change your story, your inner narrative, you choose and create a greater quality of life and a more empowered way of being.

3.) **Listen to where your heart is calling you**

44

You've lived for others for so long…now, it feels kind of odd to go in the direction your heart and Divine guidance is calling you. But know without a doubt that this particular Turning Point is very different and more powerful than all the others. This is the one where you get to decide and choose your next step, for *yourself.* You get to write an entirely new and exciting chapter for your life going forward.

People say that you're supposed to relax, settle down, and enjoy your Golden Years…Golden Years my ass!! This is the new *Golden Age*! They're going to be filled with me spreading my gold dust to every end of the earth, empowering others to embrace the sacredness of life by stepping out of fear to live the life that's calling them! I'm focused on keeping my mind sharp, my body toned and my *GrownSexy* **ooo wee** fired up for the journey! What are your plans? Will you go out of here sitting on the couch eating bon bons and watching reruns of *'The Golden Girls'* as you move into your twilight years, or will you grab this moment by the balls and ride this life out until the wheels fall off? It's your choice!

So really think about what's been tugging at your heart for so long. Do you want to realign with an old dream, start your own business, non-profit or side hustle, serve the world on a greater level, take a trip somewhere you've always wanted to go, or simply live more peacefully? What will make you happy and satisfy your Spirit, day in and day out for the remainder of your life?

_____

_____

_____      _____

_____

_____

What are your priorities? What are your likes and dislikes? What is your financial situation, does it need improving, or are you just fine? Have you lived your purpose...or do you even know what it is? Are you living your passion, or are you settling for what you think you can do, have, or become?

_____
_____
_____
_____
_____

*Fuck* those old life-crushing habits and patterns of thought and the old weary horse they rode in on! That part of your life is on *life support* and hasn't been able to move for many years.

Tomorrow is never promised; the present is a gift, and time is something you can never get back. So use your remaining time wisely!

Remember how you couldn't wait to get out of your parents' house when you turned 18, so you wouldn't have to live by their rules and you could call your own shots? Well, this feels like 18 again!! Your obligations to others are done. Your obligation to yourself is just beginning. You CAN and WILL finally, for once in your life, choose to live the life you want on your own terms!

Ask yourself the tough questions and ask God, Source Energy, the Divine (whatever your name is for your Higher power) to guide you. Trust and allow yourself to flow where you strongly feel you are being guided. You'll know without a doubt when you pay attention to your inner promptings. Use your *GrownSexyPower* to tap into the vast inner resources you have available to you and listen to and heed your *Grown Sexy Wisdom*. It is your Superpower! It will never misguide or mislead you.

Once you know, GO!

Your *Grown Sexy Wisdom* ass was made for this moment… the time is NOW for you to choose your next path and go on the most exciting leg of your journey! Follow your heart, your inner knowing, tap into your vast situational knowledge, and your creativity. Trust and have faith in yourself and in the Universe to have your back. The stars are aligning at this moment and are asking you, guided by the wisdom of the ages, to decide what beautiful and amazing direction you will choose to travel.

When you're standing at the crossroads, choosing to take the leap into greater joy, love, abundance, and freedom… remember to gleefully step inside and awaken that dormant inner child that's been in loving hibernation much of your adult life. Open up your spirit and let your soul dance and delight at the memory of all you imagined your life could be and should be. Let your heart be the guide, and prioritize from that perspective.

May this Turning Point for you be one of making a choice to let go of others' expectations for you and your life so that you have the courage to simplify and become your biggest and baddest, most authentic self….the YOU you've evolved to and will continue to evolve as.

# Chapter 3

# GrownSexySecret #2: How to Step Out of the Condition of "HOW-ITIS"

If there was one thing other than FEAR that has kept me apart from my goals and dreams, it was HOW in the heck am I going to _____? (fill in the blank)

Standing in my *GrownSexyPower*, I can clearly see that the Creator blessed me with tremendous gifts, talents, skills, and abilities, yet despite the blessing of having these enormous resources to draw from, I still had trouble figuring out what the next steps would be to get me from point A to point Z.

As I evolved throughout the years, I discovered along my journey that the question of *HOW* I was going to do it created complete overwhelm for me, because my impatient self wanted what I wanted, and I wanted it NOW!! Why should I wait? It's taken too long already! Therefore, having to think about all of the time it would take to educate myself on whatever I didn't know about my new endeavor, as well as figure out all the rest of the details required in order to pull it all together so it would be successful, was too much to handle. Anytime I felt that strong sense of overwhelm, it would stop me dead in my tracks.

So, to put it mildly, nothing of significance got done, and I sputtered out of the starting gate with my own businesses, without getting very far towards anything that looked like success. Sure, there were some fleeting successes here and there, but nothing that had any staying power.

It has taken me a lifetime to get to the point of being able to feel that I *deserve success*, simply because of my impatience and unwillingness to slow down and do the work.

Can you relate to this? Has HOW ever kept you at the starting gate, while the rest of the horses around you dash out at lightning speed, sprinting toward the finish line? Note it here:

_____

_____

_____

_____

_____

As it turns out, there was another variable missing…the one I had no idea was stalling me, nor could I even grasp prior to my Spiritual 'awakening.' That variable was my being introduced to, and gaining an understanding of, the *Law of Attraction* and how it related to my life.

You've heard of the movie *The Secret?* Well, that was my first introduction to this Universal law that *'everything is energy and what you put out you get back'* phenomenon. It's called *The Secret* because this Universal truth is what the powers that be don't want you to discover. It is the key to unlocking your inner power and changing their narrative of control over humanity. Believe me when I say this discovery was the start of a significant awakening in my life. It helped me step further into allowing my Spiritual evolution, the journey whose seeds were first planted years ago during my crazy marriage.

Talk about a wake-up call! Learning about and becoming aware of the Law of Attraction will change your life if you understand how it works and adhere to its principles. If you choose to continue doing the things you do, the same old way, this Universal law implies that you'll *keep on getting what you've always gotten,* and who wants to be saddled with that type of living for the rest of their life? Something's got to give.

Surrendering to the Universe and Universal law means that you have to be willing to let go of everything you've ever thought was dictating your life, and all the ways you've been trained to believe that life works. *You* have been the one creating your life, with every thought, belief, habit, and attitude with which you've been programmed. It has become your way of *being*.

Your circumstances? Own them. You can no longer make excuses as to why something happened a certain way…it's that way because of the *choices* you've made. If your life is full of negativity and toxicity, odds are that everything you embrace and embody perpetuates negative situations in your life. It works the other way around too. Embracing positivity, mindfulness, creating a powerful vision for your life, and living from your positive vision allow you to manifest the trappings of all good things that your happy-go-lucky vibration is in alignment with.

The root of my problem is—ok I'll admit it—I have control issues. I wanted to control being able to figure out the mechanics of the HOWS and put everything into place that would allow me to tackle all the little details I thought necessary to create what I envisioned for myself. But that's where I kept going wrong.

So, if you have a great idea or dream that's been sitting on the backburner for years, calling to you, waiting for you to bring it to life, let go of everything conventional wisdom has taught you. Here's all you need to know about busting out of HOW-itis:

## 1.) Newsflash... You Don't Have to Figure It All Out!

Ever heard of a little thing called FAITH?

**F** - *earless*
**A** - *ction*
**I** - *n Spite of*
**T** - *he*
**H** - *ere and Now?*

Faith is that area of *'unknowns'* between here and the authentic life you deserve and desire. It is that area where you create the vision and believe in the unseen with an absolute knowing that the Universe is conspiring to put things in motion for you. Start a consistent plan of action. This is the space where things start to show up to help you on your journey. The people, opportunities, money, all will start arriving on your doorstep when you learn how to allow it into your positive energetic space through the power of alignment and manifestation. Alignment means that you are in tune with your life, know what direction you want to go, and what choices will lead you down the path meant for you. Manifestation is the act of *feeling* something is yours and making it real. You are basically making it known to the Universe that whatever *it* is—a new job, car, financial freedom and so on—*will* be yours by creating the *feeling* that you already have it.

Start manifesting what you want in your life today by:

• Getting clear on what you want

- Asking the Universe for it by writing it down in a journal and/or by declaring it out loud
- Take action toward your goal
- Commit to daily visualization and feeling that you *already have it. See it in your mind's eye.*

If you aren't in tune with this, it's challenging to grasp that you can indeed create your own life by allowing Source, or Universal energy, to work on your behalf. This isn't just 'pie in the sky,' this is vision, faith, feeling, and belief all at work for you. Harness the power of the Divine…the power lives in you!!

*What would you like to manifest into your life?*

_____

_____

_____

## 2.) *Get Support.*

Navigating that area between Point A and Point Z is a bear when you don't have support. Surrounding yourself with people who support you on the journey toward your dream is paramount to actually achieving it or allowing it to fall to the wayside, another casualty of the process. There is always someone (friends, relatives, coaches, teachers, clergy) out there who believes in you and has the courage to stand with you when times are tough. These people can also provide ideas, people, places, and things that can assist you in your quest to achieve your dream. Open yourself up to share with them and allow those great things to flow to you. 'How-itis' will go running for the hills because you will have tapped into the HOW with resources that were right in front of you all along.

*Who can support you in achieving your goals and dreams?*

_____

_____

_____

## 3.) *BELIEVE!!!*

Bustin' out of the funk of HOW-itis means believing so much in what it is you want to do that you will find a way by any great and wonderful means necessary to achieve it. Refuse to 'settle' for a life of mediocrity by doing what you love to do…that thing that makes your heart sing! Believing in your dream, that vision you have for your life, will set you on a path of forward movement that will allow synchronicity to start filling in the blanks with the 'HOWs."

*Do you believe, without a doubt, in what you want for your life? Why?*

_____

_____

_____

## 4.) *Connect Yourself to the POWER of your HEART!*

The dreams you have come directly from your heart, that spirit of aliveness that drives you toward doing what it is you love to do! When you allow things into your life that you are not happy with—jobs, relationships, and other circumstances —you become disconnected from your heart. Disconnection from heart and the things that give you life is an invitation to start living more in your head as you start trying to figure out 'how' to separate yourself from those circumstances that drain the life out of you.

Connecting to your heart allows you to plug into the energy of ease and flow that will allow faith, hope, and love to create the circumstances you desire, all those 'hows' that your head wants to control and take charge of. Release yourself to your heart and watch the Universe unfold in front of your very eyes!

Remember, you have a lifetime of *Grown Sexy Wisdom* to draw from. This is your *GrownSexyPower* that helps you create the life YOU want at this stage of the game. Dream that dream and allow yourself to feel it into existence. The HOWs will all unfold before you if you let them. See it... FEEL it...Believe it...Achieve it!

*In what ways can you reconnect to the power of your heart? What makes your heart sing?*

_____

_____

_____

# Chapter 4

# Grown Sexy Secret #3: BE WILLING TO DO WHAT'S NECESSARY TO PUT YOUR LIFE ON BLAST!

*"Everything you want is out there waiting for you to ask. Everything you want also wants you. But you have to take action to get it."—**Jack Canfield***

One of the most important questions in your life at the crossroads you're faced with right now is: *are you WILLING to do what's necessary to create a life that turns you on*?

Are you done with:

- Putting yourself LAST?
- Settling for what you don't want and don't deserve?
- Putting on masks that hide your true wants, needs, and desires?

Are you ready to let go of ego and master your *authentic essence* in order to grow with a greater sense of surrender and faith in the Universe? Are you hyped about flowing into alignment with all that has been yours since your beloved birth?

First and foremost, you've got to recognize that YOU matter. Your life counts. You are here to fulfill your own soul's calling and have your own experiences in this human body so that you can evolve, transcend, transform, and ascend. You are here to learn, grow, and BE. How can you do that efficiently while being constantly tethered to what other people mandate for you?

*"You matter. Your life is not only a gift to you, but to all of us too. Your unique place in this world and your unique*

58

*personality, dreams and ideas are significant. When you wake it may feel like no one notices but one day, you'll realize that every day you stood up to take your place in the world, heaven rejoiced. Life is not always easy, but never confuse the difficult times with your own worth and significance. You matter, more than all the stars in the sky, you matter. Stand up. Be Brave. All of Heaven is Cheering you on."* – **Mick Mooney**

This powerful quote is one of my all-time favorites and is from author and longtime student of human nature, Mick Mooney. I happened to run across this on Facebook several years ago…it gives me goosebumps every time I read it!

One of the greatest gifts of transformation that has been revealed to me along this blessed spiritual journey is the realization that, throughout my entire life, I had been living everyone else's narratives for my life, but not my own. Meaning, my story and my way of being was a direct result of their stories and how I had allowed their stories to infiltrate my being through the thoughts, beliefs, habits, and attitudes that I developed as a result of being inextricably woven into the lives of all those with whom I interacted and with whom I was surrounded. It was a complex web of many layers designed from everything I'd experienced in life and had become my false identity.

I didn't realize until much later in life that this was not *my truth!* I had gotten to the place of pain where my pain now pushed me, and I was willing to do anything to let my old story go and discover who I really was.

Wow…what a profound a-ha moment! Have you ever had those moments when 'BAM' you get slapped with a huge dose of reality that simply doesn't sit well with your psyche? Have you ever thought about how much time you've spent on what everyone else wants versus what you want out of life? What's important in that moment is what you choose to do next as a result of having come to this realization.

Will you take a plate of "more of the same," or are you willing to try a new and exciting dish flavored with wonderful, amazing herbs and spices that will take your taste buds to the next level and open up the door to adding more *flava* to your life?

### Releasing the Addiction of Putting Others First

My own addiction began with what I first learned in my environment as a child. The data I observed and computed across those early years and throughout puberty, adolescence, and adulthood became the program that was running in my own life and, quite frankly, was ruining my life.

*Sample Database #1 and Subsequent Program:*

- Mom and Dad didn't get along
- Mom and Dad divorced
- Mom put her children first by going out and working herself nearly half to death to be able to provide financial support for us
- Mom suffered tremendous stress at the hands of an abusive employer to make the money she needed to continue providing for us
- Mom sacrificed her wants and needs so that our emotional, physical, and spiritual needs could be met
- Mom finally got to a point where she wanted her own life
- Mom explored what she wanted and got profoundly hurt

- Mom was at a crossroads—a major turning point
- Mom's mother, brother, and many friends died and left her alone
- Mom relinquished herself to giving up wanting anything else for herself and became deeply depressed
- As a result of lifelong stress, anxiety, and disappointments, Mom developed multiple health issues
- Mom has reverted to being obsessed with planning for her death and burial

Except for the health issues and obsessively preparing for my death, my life up to a certain point, was pretty darn close to an exact mirror of my mother's life.

I learned early on that unconditional love meant putting your children's needs before your own at all costs; I followed the program. Who knew it would be into their adulthood?

There were so many more lessons to come.

### *Sample Database #2 and Subsequent Program:*

- I was born a light-skinned Black child
- Starting in first grade, the kids began to separate me out and made fun of me for being Black
- I realized that being Black was not cool
- Boys I liked rejected me in elementary, middle, and high school because I was Black
- Our elementary school closed, and we were forced to go to an all-White neighborhood to Junior High
- The school I went to did not have students who'd been around Black people; therefore, many rejected me

- I was an athlete and played sports—I was accepted in those circles because of my talent and my academic prowess
- My Black friends I attended school with and had grown up with began to reject me, jealous of my new-found relationships in the circles I was passionate about: athletics and academics
- In High School sports and academics, the White Girls got all the attention and press, while I, though very gifted academically and as an athlete, was not the favored child…another rejection
- I felt unworthy, had low-self-esteem, and felt I always had to prove that I was just as good as or better than 'them'
- I went to college and was finally accepted by my people for who and what I was
- While I had some successes, I was ultimately rejected by the women's basketball team who embraced a white hierarchy, further damaging my self-esteem and self-worth
- Ultimately, I was married to a man who was evidently Blacker than me, because he despised me for being what he felt was too 'White' for his standards. He felt threatened by who I was and who I was becoming.

*Lord, I am just ME.*

I had put them all first and me last, to fit in and be loved, but none of them cared about *me* the person. I have been on this seesaw of acceptance and non-acceptance my entire life, depending upon the job I had, activities I chose to participate in, and who I hung around.

Ultimately to be accepted, loved, acknowledged, and

appreciated, I thought I had to keep everyone happy. Putting everyone else's needs before my own and becoming a people pleaser afraid to speak up for myself was a deeply painful experience. Never feeling like I fit in with any group, I thought I had to 'go along to get along.' This seemed like it was the best chance for me to have the friends, partnerships, and business relationships I so desired. The end result was giving away my power and suffering from a lack of confidence, low self-esteem, and resentment for years.

Add to that toxic smorgasbord the tumultuous teenage years of my two daughters and their subsequent rebellion against my authority. Plus, my penchant for hiding in the background, taking jobs where I blended in vs. standing out, afraid of being the leader I deep down yearned to be, for fear of shining my light too brightly and being rejected again. Then there were the abusive job situations where I was harassed, belittled, degraded, and unrewarded for my efforts...more rejection, unacceptance, and even lower self-esteem and self-worth. When in God's name would it all end???

All of this bloody race wrangling and finding myself in abusive situations kept me so off balance until I finally just got sick and tired of it all, threw up my hands, and made a decision. No longer was I going to care about what anyone thought about me as it related to race, or any of my other unique and complex, yet beautiful layers. As long as I alone accept, love, and appreciate all of me for who I am...all of the amazing layers that are part of my whole, I don't give a damn about what anyone else thinks! I'm too 'wise' to care anymore LOL.

*What database or program is running in your life based on*

*your life experiences?*

_____

_____

_____

_____

*How do you think this manifests in your life today?*

_____

_____

_____

_____

*How can you begin to correct these issues and move beyond your programming?*

_____

_____

_____

_____

The decision to no longer care what anyone thought about me was *huge*! It was the key to breaking my addiction to putting others first all the time. I had spent a lifetime walking a tightrope and walking on eggshells, doing things I hated, not speaking up for myself and not accepting myself for who I was. I had finally reached the point where I was open and willing to transform my life on my own terms, into what I wanted it to be for me.

The key here is…sometimes it takes years to get to the point where you are willing to change your life in order to go where you feel you are being called. Are you familiar with the quote about how a seed reaches its greatest expression?

*"For a seed to achieve its greatest expression, it must come completely undone. The shell cracks, its insides come out and EVERYTHING CHANGES. To someone who doesn't understand GROWTH, it would look like complete DESTRUCTION."* – **Cynthia Occelli**

That's some damn powerful stuff! Change is often such a difficult thing because it causes us to get uncomfortable and, after all, our bodies and minds seek comfort and routine, while our spirits want to soar. That's where the imbalance causes dis-ease in your body. Why would you want to step out into that big scary world and actually do something that causes you to become completely undone?

Because IT'S WORTH IT! YOU'RE WORTH IT! YOUR LIFE IS WORTH IT! Someone out there needs what you have to give if you are willing to serve. Unless you are willing to become completely undone and make yourself uncomfortable, growth and change cannot occur, and your dreams are likely to stay on lockdown. At this point in time, are you willing to allow that to happen?

Are you finally *willing* to put you *first*? Now is the time to go where you have not been willing to go before. Life is short, and tomorrow is never promised. You cannot get back time that you feel you've wasted…it's gone forever. This is serious business, so serious I have a 'deathbed' meditation that I use in my coaching program that always creates profound shifts in perspective for many of my clients. During this meditation, I have you reflect back over your life, imagining yourself on your deathbed, as you take a journey back to all the things you *coulda, shoulda, woulda* done. All the chances you didn't take, things you left unfinished or never even tried. Think about the times you didn't allow yourself to *get out of your own way* so you could play full out and live the joyful, abundant life you deserved. Then, I have you imagine the intense regret you *feel* in that moment as a result. When you feel it, that's when it becomes so real for you. Talk about powerful—it's truly an eye opener. Can you imagine your life passing before your eyes and the feeling of regret in that moment? Make a vow to yourself right now, *to live life fully*. The only time that matters is the present. Know without a doubt that you already have everything you need for the rest of your journey inside you, which is why understanding and tapping into your *Grown Sexy Wisdom* is your life force energy in this moment.

So, crack open your beautiful seed and allow yourself to fully blossom!

You have the skills, gifts and talents, life lessons, experience, situational knowledge, values, creativity, authenticity, and soul, all wrapped up in that beautiful, strong, and sexy package that is you! Your *Grown Sexy Wisdom* is your *GrownSexyPower*, the beautiful essence of who you are including that confident sexy swagger you have in the face of what would bring most people to their knees.

Your *Grown Sexy Wisdom* is your birthright and your *truth*. What an invaluable treasure chest filled with all the golden nuggets necessary to help you create the greater life you want for yourself. All you need to do is let go and go with the FLOW! Imagine your life on steroids…more fun, more joy, more happiness and abundance, more fulfillment, more energy…it's a win-win-win…if you are willing to GO!

Now, pay attention…I'm driving this point home because it's so important. *If you choose not to go, you will continue*

66

*paying the price in your health, happiness, and well-being.*

Want to know how not heeding your heart's call is affecting you?

*Pay attention to the SIGNS.*

If you are feeling out of balance in any area of your body-mind-spirit, that's a good indicator that you are disconnected from your truth, the heart and soul of who you are, and all the ways it wants to express itself that you typically suppress. I have a very cool mantra for living that grew out of resolving my addiction to putting others first and putting me last. I call this mantra *'honor your sacred triad.'*

# YOUR SACRED TRIAD

*Honoring your Sacred Triad* means to become consciously aware of your emotions, thoughts, beliefs, habits, and attitudes, so you can *feel* when these are affecting your body-mind-spirit. With this newfound awareness, you can begin to address those parts of your Triad that are feeling out of sync and need self-care and healing. Then, through self-love and non-judgment, you can begin to release and heal whatever is causing your imbalance, transforming it into a way of being that nourishes and replenishes your sacred divine feminine energy—part of the foundation of your *Grown Sexy Wisdom*. This is the seat of your *GrownSexyPower*, the essence of who you are, and deserves your utmost love, nurturing, and attention.

### *Ways you can tell you are out of sync:*

**BODY**: If your body is lethargic, sickly, inflammed, obese, you have any organ dysfunction, pain…your physical being is telling you your MIND & SPIRIT are out of whack.

**MIND**: if you are feeling like a victim, apathetic, depressed, resentful, hateful, unhappy, unsatisfied, unable to control your emotions, and are a reactionary to circumstances in your life, your BODY and SPIRIT will react negatively, and you'll totally feel out of balance.

**SPIRIT**: If you have a longing to follow a dream that has gone unfulfilled, or feel that life has little meaning, your BODY and MIND will also be off kilter.

Your *Sacred Triad* is your being's center of balance and well-being. The body-mind-spirit are all interconnected, so when one aspect of your Sacred Triad is out of balance, it causes dysfunction in your entire center of energy.

When you are loving what you do and doing what you love, following your heart and daring to live life on your terms, it creates a synergy within your temple that can help you manage stress and deal with challenges better. Feelings of happiness, love, satisfaction, and positivity cause your cells

68

to vibrate higher which creates an overall feeling of well-being in your body. Have you ever heard the quote "When you give up your dream, you die"? Not stepping out of your comfort zone, thinking negatively, and having a defeatist attitude will cause your cells to vibrate at a lower vibrational frequency, which can lead to dis-ease in your body and potentially cause health issues. Doing what you love allows your happy hormones to fire up, which in turn helps reduce the stress response in multiple areas of your life. So, serving others and doing work that is more fulfilling and in alignment with your values, morals, and integrity, surrounding yourself with people who are on the same wavelength as you, and expressing your *Grown Sexy Wisdom* in the creative and authentic way that only you can, will allow the body to feel good and lessen the effects of stress in your life. Sing that song your soul wants to sing! When your soul sings, your body sings, and all of your cells sing! When you are miserable, defeated, stressed out, and depressed, your cells start to feel bad. For God's sake, now is the time to do what you LOVE…your health and happiness depends on it!

## A Victim of Victimhood

I have never seen such a vivid example of the damage caused from being a victim of life, refusing to choose for oneself, and maintaining a low vibrational system of belief as a former friend of mine, who I'll call Marci to protect her privacy.

Marci was the mother of 5 children, all adults in their 20s, all the unwilling victims of an extremely abusive marriage. She had also been the product of a broken home growing up, where she was the oldest of 5 siblings. When I met her, she was suffering from extremely low self-esteem, an inability to make decisions, paranoia, and quite a bit of PTSD from the treatment she was subjected to for over 25 years by a narcissistic, psychopathic, abusive husband. Her life was in tatters as a result of being with this man, who took an already fragile self-esteem and obliterated it, further destroying her on multiple levels: physically, mentally, verbally and emotionally.

A mere shell of the up-and-coming woman she once was, Marci had lived in the 'comfortable pain' of her dysfunctional marital relationship for far too long. She started to believe the narrative old dude had created for her life. His story for her was that she was a horrible wife and mother. He sold her on a false story that negated any of his true responsibility for any of the problems in their marriage and family. Mentally, physically and emotionally he drummed this into her head until she started to believe it. Everything related to why their kids turned out the way they did was her fault. She was not only a horrible mother and horrible wife, she was overall just a general piece of shit to him, worthless in every way. He never bypassed the opportunity to let her know how awful she was.

Feeling deeply depressed from the heavy guilt that her mentally and emotionally bankrupt spouse laid at her feet during his years of abuse, and without the intestinal fortitude or courage to leave the marriage on her own, Marci suffered tremendously. She was eventually forced to divorce him based on a heinous set of circumstances he set into motion, leaving her no alternative. Despite the divorce that he initiated and finalized, Marci continued living in the marital home with him. Part of the reason she stayed was because she embraced the massive guilt she felt for *'fucking up the kids'* because she'd allowed herself to stay in that marriage without the courage to leave. She was truly living his narrative for her, but she was so desperately in need of love, affection, appreciation, and acknowledgement, she still pined over him, longing for his love and affection.

As one of her oldest and dearest friends, it was hard for me to fathom her continuing to submit herself to such torture, but what I understood clearly was that Marci was scared to death of leaving the only life she'd ever known, even though it was intensely dysfunctional. In her pain, she had become comfortable, afraid of pursuing anything outside that situation that might allow her to live happily. She continued to hold on with a death grip to her dysfunctional adult children, who had now begun being abusive to her. She insisted she was staying in the home because she had nowhere else to go.

In diving deeper with Marci, she longed for a greater life but didn't know how to let go of the narrative that had defined her. It would have been like losing her identity to choose to cut the umbilical cord.

Marci had a favorite sister, whom she adored, who lived in Pensacola, Florida near the Gulf. Marci enjoyed visiting every chance she got because she absolutely loved the beach and the peace and serenity she found there. It was there that she also found the missing pieces of herself and enjoyed a harmonious new way of being. Her sister loved her so much, she wanted to be her advocate, her freedom fighter, and tried so hard for several years to try to get her to let go and choose a happier life, all to no avail. Marci didn't know who she was any longer and refused to give herself permission to be happy. She instead settled for being less than what she was capable of being and deprived herself of everything she knew would make her happy. It was almost as if she was punishing herself for the guilt her ex-husband continued to rain down on her about her faults, not his, as it related to their marriage and family.

Marci was a victim living in perpetual victimhood. Her soul had become numb, and she paid the price with poor health, mentally, and physically.

It pained me to see her this way, but she was a clear example of someone who was miserable and suffered in body-mind-spirit for refusing to choose the life that she knew would make her happy. Being a victim was all she'd ever known, proof that, for some, it's not easy to go where you are being called. But make a mental note…it *is possible* with a shift in mindset and a willingness to want to change. With the right guidance, you can move beyond your fears!

It's always a ***choice***. I myself have been a victim at times, but I came to a point where I refused to continue to allow myself to be in perpetual victimhood. I had to come to terms with myself once I became aware of what my issue was and could identify what belief system had been holding me back. I knew if I wanted to rewrite my story in order to move forward into creating the greatest chapter of my life, I had to do the shadow work. This meant taking a good, hard but non-judgmental look at all my dark places and learning how to sync them with my light places. Doing this would allow my light to shine as brightly as possible, so that others could shine. That is my destiny, and that is my purpose.

That is my choice.

If you've been a victim in the past, know that it was in the past. Don't give the past a seat at the table of your present.

You cannot change the past. Learn to be grateful for the lessons that it taught you, that have become part of your badass *Grown Sexy Wisdom*. In this moment, you have the choice whether to live as a victim today, tomorrow and the rest of your days. How will you respond?

What will you choose at this crossroads? The same old narrative that's been flatlining in your subconscious, sabotaging every chance at a more blissful and satisfying life, or will you reach for your highest self...the Divine Feminine Being that you are with all of your unique and powerful *Grown Sexy Wisdom* to guide you?

Are you now at the point where you are ***willing*** to create a life that turns you on...the greater life that's calling to you?

If you are willing to take the plunge...let's dive in!

### Thoughts and Words Have Power

This is where the rubber meets the road. Are you ready for your greater journey? From here on out, I'm going to get a little "woo-woo" on you. I'm going to show you how your Spiritual self or true essence plays into all of this. Believe me, it only seems "woo woo" if you've never allowed yourself to learn, understand, and open your Sacred Triad to who you truly are. So, hang on as we explore this some more!

As I've shared earlier, your *Grown Sexy Wisdom* is the foundation and the essence of all that you are, everything you have evolved to and the wisdom you will use to continue your evolution and ascension for the rest of your earthly life. Woven within the mix of this intricately beautiful treasure that is you is your highest self, or the part of you that is wise, aware, and connected to all that *is*. Your *Grown Sexy Wisdom* and your highest self go hand-in-hand.

If you've merely scratched the surface of who you are, at first, it might be a bit challenging for you to understand that, besides your mind and body, there is a spiritual essence to your human beingness that also guides you. My purpose in life is to reconnect you to your sacred truth, your CORE... that I call your

**C** - *enter*
**O** - *f*
**R** - *adiant*
**E** - *nergy*

As psychologist Athena Laz explains in her blog post, "What Actually Is A 'Higher Self' & How Do I Connect To Mine?"(mindbodygreen.com, October 5, 2020):

"The Highest Self, or just the Self, can be defined as our inner guidance that is separate from our personality (Ego Self). It is the connector of the material and the mystical; the Universe within that dictates our experience as embodied beings. (The word embodied reminds us that we are more than just our physicality—we are our spiritual essence too.) In other words, your highest self has nothing to do with your ego. Your highest self communicates with you (internally, passively, receptively) through your imagination, meditations, and dreams via personal symbols, and externally/actively through collective symbols: stories, tarot, myth, ritual and prayer.

In layman's terms, your highest self is an extension of yourself that is part of you and part of your Higher Power (God, Source Energy, whatever it is for you). This sacred energy, which we all have, links us to everyone and everything. We can use our Highest Self to connect to the higher consciousness within us, the universal wisdom, power and knowledge from within."

When you are In alignment with your Higher Self, you are in tune with your soul. From this place you can experience your Divine Feminine energy and become more aware of your part in this interconnected world. This is your TRUTH. Your *Grown Sexy Wisdom* and your Highest Self combined equal a *GrownSexyPower* that, once fully realized and unleashed, will allow you to see greater possibilities and opportunities for your life. Now, you can express your greatest potential by following your heart and trusting your inner guidance. This will give you a sense of peace and well-being unlike any you've ever experienced before, *if you are willing to see beyond* all that your limited ego-mind has been conditioned to believe, and allow yourself to see it, feel it, believe it, and receive it.

So, just what is the secret to making this next and greatest chapter the *golden age* of your life? You've paid your dues. NOW is the time when you get to choose for *you* a life of happiness, abundance, love, and freedom unlike any you've ever allowed yourself to fully experience before. If you're feelin' your *Grown Sexy Wisdom* self, you know you weren't meant to sit on the sidelines watching the game, going through the motions in life...not you, Sis! You were born with a fire in your heart and have overcome tremendous odds to get to this place. You are standing on the edge of your freedom. Let's just say that right now you're putting mediocre living on notice.

As I was coming into my own power, I chose another very important, life-affirming, personal mantra that guides my everyday living, which is *'average is NOT in my blood!'* I even designed my own affirmation T-shirt around it as a powerful reminder. For once in my life, I began loving and accepting the many layers of me, the amazing soul who came into this life at 2 lbs. 15 oz—2 months early! I have always had a knowing, for as long as I can remember, that there was so much more in life I was supposed to do, but due to the circumstances in which I grew up, and subsequent beliefs I developed, I held myself apart from my destiny for most of my adult life. Despite the times I have held myself back, I've also had moments where I took tremendous strides forward all because *I know who I am* and refused to settle for anything less than who I am. I know, what a paradox, right? But this is what has worked for me. If you're human, you know we've all had times where we have stood in our brilliance and other times where we've wondered *what the hell am I doing?*

Before I get into the meat and potatoes of this section…let's take time to define your own personal mantra, as I believe this is a powerful tool for transforming your way of being.

A *mantra* is like a personal slogan or philosophy for your life. It is a potent reminder of who you are and serves as words to live by.

Some examples are:

- 'My body is a temple'
- Nike's 'Just Do It'
- 'All is Well Right Here and Now'

Take a few minutes right now, close your eyes, and take a deep cleansing breath....ahhhh! What personal mantra can you create for yourself that will guide your life force energy from this point forward? You can make it as simple or complex as you'd like, but the easier it is to remember, the more you will likely commit to repeating it and devoting the time to do it.

**My Personal Mantra**:

_____

_____

Repeat it out loud in the first 5 minutes you wake up every morning and the last 5 to 10 minutes before you go to sleep in the evening. Those are the two most important times in your entire day. Each of those moments sets the tone for how you begin your day, and subsequently, the life affirming thoughts you want to ingrain into your subconscious while you are sleeping. Try it for 30 days...that's the amount of time it usually takes to transform your way of thinking. By sticking with this schedule, pretty soon, you will have retrained your brain and programmed yourself to be unstoppable!

Now that you have an awesome new tool for reprogramming your subconscious into kickass mode, let's dive into my dynamic strategy for taking your *Grown Sexy Wisdom* self to the next level!!

## VICA: The Grown Sexy Sacred Strategy for Going Where Your Highest Self is Calling!

Are you aware of what gets in your way of attaining the greater life you desire for yourself, the life that turns you on and puts your life on full BLAST?

If you haven't quite been able to put your finger all the way on it, here are several reasons that may be causing you to sabotage your ability to turn up your wattage...

1.) You don't have a VISION for your life. You live life day to day focused on your circumstances, being a reactionary to everything that happens in your life vs being a visionary. A visionary creates a vision for their life and allows it to guide and pull them forward rather than letting their circumstances guide them.

2.) You don't know **how** to get started

3.) You aren't **aware** of what's holding you back and how to shift the program

4.) You aren't aware of the *GrownSexyPower* of your *Grown Sexy Wisdom* and your ability to create the life you want for yourself

5.) You aren't aware that you **create** your life every day, with the thoughts you think, your inner and outer self-talk, habits and beliefs

6.) You aren't connected to your **heartspace**, where the answers to all you want in life reside

There is a simple 4-step strategy for getting out of your own way and masterfully allowing all that you desire that I use with my coaching clients called the *VICA Strategy ™*.

# V-I-C-A =

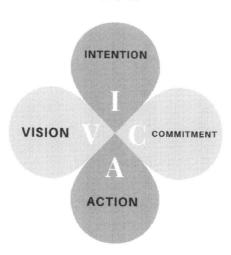

**V** Creating a **VISION** for your life sets the Universe in motion to bring you the people, places, things, and circumstances that will guide you on your journey toward achieving the life you dream of. A powerful vision sets the stage for allowing you to release your old stories and allows in the life that has always been possible for you, the one you've been unable to see or realize until now.

**I** Setting an **INTENTION** changes the game. Instead of allowing life to happen to us daily, as we bounce from circumstance to circumstance, setting an intention activates our receptivity (Universal Antenna) to be able to manifest what we intend to attract and call into our lives. There is much power behind setting an intention.

**C** Making a **COMMITMENT** to ourselves and others who we manifest to assist us in our journey will allow us to achieve our goals vs. just paying lip service to our growth and ascension. Committing to your journey and showing gratitude for those who show up to help you will create more positive experiences and situations that will accelerate the manifestation of your vision. Let your integrity shine!

**A** Finally, the main cog of this strategy that shows the Universe you are serious about what you intend to create is **ACTION**! Action is the force that sets it all off and is what will allow all the HOWs to start showing up. It is sheer ecstasy when you begin to see your life's path Divinely unfold in front of you! What massive action are you committing to take in order to achieve your vision, the greater life you intend to create for yourself? Nothing will happen if you do nothing. Learn to take action *before you are ready*!

Most of us know how to make a commitment and take action but may find it a little confusing creating a vision or setting an intention. Allow me to clarify those two a little better for you.

### How to Create A VISION for your Life

*"Create the highest, grandest vision for your life, because you become what you believe."* – **Oprah Winfrey**

Creating a compelling vision for the life you want for yourself creates clarity for where you want your life to go; it's basically like creating a roadmap, a direction for you to travel on the road toward your personal and professional goals and dreams. If you never take the time to create a vision for your life, it leaves you susceptible to living in the past and falling victim to other people's wishes and whims for you and your life, leaving you apt to continue living someone else's narrative, rather than creating your own.

When considering what you want your vision to be, give yourself permission to go BIG or go HOME! Don't consider anything off limits or impossible! Focus on what you want that would be most fulfilling for you, not on what you *don't want*. What's your endgame...is it love, peace, and happiness, or wealth? What legacy do you want to leave? Ask yourself thought-provoking questions across all areas of your life to determine what's important to you so that you can begin seeing all the different possibilities available.

Here's the one I was asked when I started out creating my own vision on the journey toward creating my greatest life: *"What would you do if money were no issue, and you knew you could not fail?"* This question virtually leaves nothing out because money and failure are two of the biggest obstacles to people believing they can achieve their dreams. If those two are taken out of the equation, it makes it easier to craft a vision as well as transform your mindset.

So, pick a day, right now, don't procrastinate! Schedule something on your calendar, some quiet time for yourself for an hour or two to bring your vision to life. If it helps, you can even meditate beforehand, light some incense...get into your Zen mode, grab your favorite notebook or journal and begin the greatest work of self-love you've ever done for yourself.

If you really want to nail it down and need a little more guidance, here is an excellent visualization method I've used for creating my own vision. This will help you get amazingly clear on what you want for your life.

Let's begin by visualizing where you want to go. What do you want your life to look like in the next 3 years? Here are 10 questions to use as your guide. Once you're finished visualizing, write down everything you want your life to look like by thoughtfully and specifically answering each question.

1. What legacy do you want to leave to your family or, even bigger, the world?

_____
_____
_____
_____

2. How do you want to serve others?

_____
_____
_____
_____

3. What type of relationships do you have?

_____
_____
_____
_____

4. What skills or experience do you have that can bring your vision to life?

_____
_____
_____
_____

5. What gifts and talents do you possess that would make you happiest if you were using them daily?

_____
_____
_____

6. Where do you want to be financially?

_____

_____

_____

_____

7. Where do you want to live that would set your soul on fire?

_____

_____

_____

_____

8. What makes you feel most satisfied, happy and fulfilled?

_____

_____

_____

_____

9. What do you want more of in your life?

_____

_____

_____

_____

10. What would your life look like if you lived with no regrets?

_____

_____

_____

_____

Use these answers to craft your vision and create your unique roadmap to your goals and dreams. Remember, this doesn't have to be static. As you evolve and your priorities change, so will your vision. Simply go back and tweak it when necessary and keep on your merry way!

## Setting your intention

Everything that happens in the Universe begins with an intention. Intentions are the creative power behind the fulfillment of your wildest goals and dreams; intention allows you to bring your vision to life! It is the fertile seed for what you want to create in your life that allows the energy of the Universe to bring it to fruition.

I believe that setting an intention is a sacred process and a sacred skill to master. So, just how do we go about mastering this powerful method for allowing our deepest desires?

Here is a simple guide for setting the energy of intention into motion:

1.) **Practice Meditation** – Meditation works in so many instances. It allows you to be still and focus on your breath, in order for you to tap into the depths of your consciousness. In this stillness, you can transcend the ego-mind and sow the seeds of intention.

2.) **Listen to your Highest Self** – In the stillness of meditation or prayer, focus on listening to the whispers, the words, thoughts and images that come through your heart. Here you will gain the clarity you seek for your path forward. Acknowledge it, listen to it, and heed those sacred promptings.

3.) **Write Down Your Intentions** – When writing them down, be sure to be as *specific* as possible! Letting the Universe know exactly what you intend to create for your life will set it in motion to bring you those things.

4.) **Use a Decisive Manner for Reciting Your Intention** – Use words like, I AM prosperous and abundant, I AM healthy and strong…speak these words out loud as if you've already created it or already have it. Your words have the power to create your life by speaking your intention into existence.

5.) **Let Go, Have Faith, and Allow the Outcome** – Don't spend your time lamenting about when or how your Intention will come to fruition, you only create resistance and slow down the process by doing so. Set it and forget it! Let go, take consistent action toward what you wish to create, and allow the Universe to work its Divine magic!

For me, intention is an extension of my daily meditation or my prayer. You can set intentions as often as you'd like— daily, weekly, monthly, yearly, it's totally up to you. It's simply a matter of determining what you wish to create, asking your Higher Power to help you create it, and allowing that Divine power to go to work for you.

A few years ago, I learned to shift into setting New Year's Intentions vs. New Year's Resolutions. A New Year's Intention is a powerful statement of how you intend for your year to unfold. It is a smaller goal with intended actions that sets Universal energy in motion to help bring it to fruition. A New Year's Resolution is typically a big goal set forth to fix a problem in your life. One such resolution that people make is to lose weight. Not achieving this resolution tends to make you feel like a failure.

The very first year I made the change, it was like this huge vortex of energy was released, and so many incredible things started happening in my life. The specific intention I set at the stroke of midnight that New Year's Eve going into 2018 was: "*I intend to let go of everything that isn't in my Highest Good and doesn't serve my Highest Self.*" It wasn't long after setting that intention that the Universe released me from a very abusive job situation I had been in for 10 years. This experience showed me that when you speak an intention and have faith in the unseen, this will have a powerful effect on the trajectory of your life. Try it for yourself going into the next New Year!

**Be Willing to Invest in Yourself**

In order to get to where you want to go, sometimes you've got to admit to yourself that you need a little help. What better way to add more gold dust to our *Grown Sexy Wisdom* coffers than to keep our hearts and minds open to learning and growing on new and exciting levels throughout our lives?

This is something I had to come to grips with during my own entrepreneurial journey. There was a point where I realized that I couldn't do everything I wanted to do *by myself*. I simply did not have the expertise in certain areas of business that I sorely needed. Wow, was that so hard for me! My ego fought like hell against asking for help because I had always been self-sufficient and independent since my teenage years. With all the different jobs I'd held, I lauded myself as a 'jack of all trades' in a variety of disciplines. I thought for sure I could start, run, and be successful at a business. But, Sis...did I find out that I was dead wrong.

When you start a business or any new pursuit that stretches

you out of your comfort zone to that extent, believe me, every limiting belief that has ever held you back will rise to the surface, like the foam on a good head of beer. Wallowing in that stew of overwhelm, inaction, indecision, and fear of failure undermined the pursuit of my dreams. I didn't feel like I was good enough or capable enough to achieve my goals or to make my own income.

So I had to have the courage to ask for help. For me, that meant transcending my ego and admitting that I wasn't great at everything. It was the best decision I made in my entire life. Good Lord, how often do we hold ourselves back from success because we try to be fiercely independent or because we are control freaks?

Having been an athlete since grade school, I recognize the value of a coach who can bring out the treasure that is buried in you, allowing you to excel in the pursuit of your passion. That's what you need at times: a coach, mentor, or guide who can help you navigate the chasm between point A and point Z...better yet, a coach who can build a bridge to help you get to your goals faster, because they've already navigated the chasm!

But you've got to be willing to invest in *you*. In this consumer-based world, we spend money on so many other things we *want*...that cup of daily Starbucks, a new big-screen TV, the latest iPhone, but for some reason, we stop short when it comes to spending money on something we *need* that could vastly improve our lives.

Imagine the value in taking the time to determine your VICA strategy. What help would you need that could take your life to an entirely different level so you can achieve your vision?

So, instead of buying more things that *you want*…start to think about what *you really need*. Begin to invest in yourself and get the help you need to achieve your goals and a quality of life beyond anything you could ever imagine. Determine what value you place on your life and all the experiences you would love to have. Does that value go beyond your TV or coffee cup?

So take a seat, quiet your mind and take some sacred *GrownSexyME* time for yourself, to summarize your own personal VICA strategy. What is your sacred vision? What intention will you set to put things in motion? What is your personal commitment to yourself, and what consistent action are you willing to take to get you there? I promise you, taking this action now will start to empower you, because you will walk away with a powerful vision that gives you a renewed passion for life.

*What is your **VISION** for your Life?*

_____

_____

_____

_____

*What **INTENTIONS** will you set to put your vision in motion?*

_____

_____

_____

_____

*Write down your personal **COMMITMENT** to yourself*

_____

_____

_____

_____

*What consistent **ACTION** are you willing to take to bring your vision to fruition?*

_____

_____

_____

_____

The VICA Strategy will positively get you reconnected to your CORE, as well as embracing and applying your sacred *Grown Sexy Wisdom* to your life. It is your innermost *GrownSexyPower* that will help you live from a stronger, more purposeful and inspired perspective and will transform both your mind and your heartset. The ultra-beautiful part about this strategy is that it will give you an ability to see new and exciting possibilities and opportunities for your life and allow you the determination and drive to begin to act on them.

Applying this strategy, which will become your personal game plan for empowering you to hold your focus as you take action toward your vision, is the secret sauce that gives you permission to stay committed to creating your own destiny and to be consistent in bringing your vision to life!

As a coach and mentor...I have been exactly where you are. I would not be where I am today without asking for and accepting help, as well as taking action to implement the steps I've learned. I can help you navigate the crossroads and elevate to a new and exciting chapter that is all about *you*. You deserve to love the life you live, prosper beyond your wildest dreams, and love with a renewed energy! It's all about you, baby...embrace your *GrownSexyWisdom* and live the life of freedom that fully expresses your truth!

# Chapter 5

# GrownSexySecret #4: Success Happens When You DECIDE!

*If you keep on doing the same things you've always done, you'll keep on getting the same things you've gotten.*
**– Unknown**

No truer words have ever been spoken.

There's also this: *"The definition of insanity is doing the same thing, over and over again, expecting a different result."* **– Albert Einstein**

Take a moment, stand back, close your eyes and *feel* the essence of all that is YOU. Bring into your awareness everything about you that *is* your amazing life…all the love, the lightness, the darkness, the laughter, the pain, the lessons, the sorrows, the experiences, as well as your gifts/talents and skills. All of your pure and amazing gold dust! Wrap yourself in the amazing strength of your *GrownSexyWisdom*, your unique *GrownSexyPower*…and allow it to permeate your entire being… body-mind-spirit. See yourself as the powerful, confident, sexy, resourceful, loving being that you are. Your sexiness, that aura of quiet strength, confidence, serenity and peace that surrounds you and follows you wherever you go, that makes you irresistible to others without you even having to utter a word.

That is who you are, unique Goddess! Own every dazzling, brilliant, and delectable layer that is YOU! Knowing all of this and standing in your power…is there nothing you can't do?

You are standing at the precipice of your freedom, baby.

92

What path will you choose for yourself? What will you fully and completely commit yourself to?

This is who you are…this is your life! *Now* is your moment! Success—whatever that means for you—happens when *you* decide. If you want more abundance, love, freedom, or joy, it can be yours. Know that you deserve it. I'll say it over and over again: you've **earned the right** to express your *GrownSexySelf* in all its *GrownSexyGlory*. This is your time to shine!

You are the creator and owner of your unique vision. It will not create itself, so don't waste another second putting it on the backburner again. Procrastination will set the Universe in motion to bring you more of *that*. At this stage in life, who wants to delay success and satisfaction? I'm a firm believer in and a student of the Law of Attraction. I believe that when you put things off, the Universe is going to mirror that back to you…and guess what? It will take longer to manifest the life you desire because if it's not your priority, it isn't the Universe's priority to bring it to you either.

It took a blasted 56 years of my precious presence here on earth to finally **decide** the life I wanted for myself. I procrastinated the hell out of making decisions for me, that's why it's taken me so loooong! Heck, I knew in my 20s that I didn't want to play the corporate game. I despised it, but I didn't quite know what I wanted to do or have the courage to do whatever *it* was. I did, however, carry a knowing within me that I was supposed to be way more than I was allowing myself to be. I remember being in my late 20s and in counseling due to the depression I experienced because of my marriage and being confused about who I was, what I wanted, and my path forward. I was on and off antidepressants for years, struggling with what I now know was an inability to cope with settling for living a life less than what I wanted for myself.

I knew deep down that my life could be different. My intuition kept telling me that my way of being was not the life for me, but sure enough…that's the path I chose at the time even though I *hated it*. I simply wasn't ready. I was standing in my fear, lack of self-esteem, hunger for love and acceptance and surrounded by competing narratives for my life, trying to do anything else but meld into the matrix. Wife, mother, job, home responsibilities, all I knew was I needed to have and maintain a job and needed to bring in an income in order to have the things I wanted and needed, and after my babies were born, to be able to provide for them.

After going through the motions, putting everyone else first, settling for less than, playing small and hiding my gifts and talents, it took being in a highly abusive work environment in my mid-40s to allow me to discover my purpose.

Suddenly one evening, it was as if all the buzzers, bells, and whistles finally went off in my mind, saying, *'enough, enough…no mas!!'* I can't take it anymore! And just like that, BAM, it slapped me right smack in my face as I lay in bed with my boyfriend contemplating life one starry night. In that moment, I DECIDED that I was tired of being less than I was capable of being, and done with being treated like everyone's beeyotch. I DECIDED that I was VALUABLE. I DECIDED that I was *not* going to accept 'less than' living any longer, because I realized I had been going through the motions in life, standing on the sidelines watching life pass me by! It was my time to *'get in the game'* and show what I was made of!

94

What I discovered was my TRUTH and what I have always been made of: heart, soul, substance, and integrity, as well as a unique and powerful spirit with a deep love for humanity and a longing to serve others on a grand scale. In that moment, I was being called forth to empower others to allow themselves to live the greater life that is their birthright and that they are fully capable of living with the natural extraordinary talents they were gifted at birth. In a flash, I became keenly aware of my gifts, talents, skills, and passions, as well as the courage that had always been there but had laid dormant during the times I failed to consistently tap into it along my journey.

The reason I heard the Divine prompting at that Divine time is because the Universe (God) saw that, at that point in my evolution, my heart and mind had been opened to fully receive the message. I was ready to take action. After all my life lessons and everything I'd learned, earned and been burned at, I was now ready, with a treasure chest full of *Grown Sexy Wisdom*, to serve others on a major level.

My Divine purpose was to help others *get off the sidelines and into the game*, no longer going through the motions in life, and to dare to live their passions with no fear, no excuses, and no regrets! That was when my life coaching mentor showed me that the best way to serve was to become a life coach, which she fully believed I was more than capable of doing. Then, voila…in September of 2009, my very first business was born!

But what would I name this fledgling business? Having been a basketball player with a life-long passion for the game that helped me learn how to transcend my negative thoughts and circumstances and achieve my goals, I came up with the name "GotNXT." GotNXT became known as *a movement to empower you to no longer be a slave to going through the motions in life, powered by thoughts, habits, and beliefs that no longer serve you. Now is the time to get off the sidelines and into the game, powered by your N-X-T, Natural— Xtraordinary—Talents, stepping out of your comfort zone and into the life you were destined to live from the day you were born!"* Powerful, ain't it?

But…while I had tons of fun, loads of intermittent successes, spent a shitload of money…(sometimes even paying for others to attend my events), promoting and selling my empowerment gear, and feeding my need to feel successful, I wasn't. Not monetarily by any means. I didn't have the knowledge or the courage I needed to figure out the quickest path to consistent revenue. It was almost as if I didn't want to be successful. Have you ever had that feeling before? "OMG, *what if I make it?"*

GotNXT temporarily fulfilled my need to feel like I was on my way to the mountaintop, and my passion for serving others. But I still struggled with the many masks I wore beneath the confident facade: the mask of fear, low self-esteem and self-worth, fear of success and failure and an inability to figure out how to market my business for maximum success. I was afraid of being successful, because people might actually like me, or conversely, they might actually hate me and see me as a phony. Lord, did I have a bad case of Imposter Syndrome.

As I shared my GotNXT 'living my passion' space with my day job that was literally sucking the life force from me, I had some brilliant and courageous moments in the midst of the tug of war. It was during that time that a series of events in the economy led to me working out a deal with my boss that allowed me the ability to work from home. That was a Godsend in so many ways. It meant I no longer had to make the 86-mile daily roundtrip to and from the office. It also freed me from having to be in the midst of the negativity, condescension, and perverseness of the management team and gave me the freedom I needed to begin to see different possibilities for my life.

This newfound freedom was amazing! I also attracted a love interest, who happened to work for an airline. He knew that I needed a break from all the stress and strain I was under raising my teens and working in a place I was deeply unsatisfied with. He had the brilliant idea to add me to his flight benefits, and the rest was history. One weekend, he totally surprised me and said, "I'm putting us on a plane to Miami." I tried to fight it, because I hadn't been on a plane since 1984 out of fear of flying. But, I took the chance to say YES, and you better believe that changed my entire life.

My friend had opened me up to an entire new world of adventure, all because I DECIDED to say YES to conquering my fear of flying. He opened my heart, mind, and spirit to a whole new way of living by feeding my sense of adventure and my desire to feel like I was special to someone. His generosity allowed me to feel loved, appreciated, acknowledged, and desired. I was on top of the world!

During that same time, I had also reconnected with a dear childhood friend of mine who lived in California. I made several trips there, and since my daughters had also been added to the flight benefits, they too got to travel with us sometimes. I fell in love with Cali. It felt so new, fresh, and exciting…and I was drawn to it on a spiritual level, feeling that this was the place the Divine wanted me to be in order to grow and expand. So, after my last trip in June of 2012, I decided that I loved the possibilities California had to offer so much that I went home and put my house on the market. Within two months, I had packed up the contents of my house in a U-Haul and was Cali bound for good!!!

How's that for a big sissy LOL?

That big sissy is not who I am...it was the farthest thing from my *truth*. I had proved that hundreds of times in my life. I just couldn't shake the belief system that rocked me to my core.

Although I love Cali and still reside here, it certainly didn't turn out to fully be the land of milk and honey I had imagined. I went through further growing pains with my daughters, boundary setting with people who took advantage of my kindness, dating, and getting used to my new surroundings.

After a series of challenges surrounding the adult friendship with my childhood friend, I ended up dissolving our friendship for good in 2019. It didn't turn out to be anything like I thought it would be, and I could see that although we fantasized for decades about living out our lives together, it was headed for disaster. We were not the same children anymore; we were two grown women, with two different perspectives on life, each with an ego the size of Texas. I also found it hard to stay immersed in her fears and insecurities... it frustrated the daylights out of me to continue trying to help my closest friends and family to elevate themselves to the greater level they wanted to move toward in word only, but not in deed, due to fear.

At the same time, I began to understand that I was going to end up traveling this journey alone. Dear God, was it hard— between sharing a home with my two daughters who unleashed 'Rebellion-Part 2: The California Version,' dropping my best friend, and working for a company that was still continuing to rip the life from my heart. Dating men proved to be a challenge too. Most had a need for lust versus love, so at some point, something had to give. I was drowning in a sea of depression, resentment, parental pain and loneliness. I went on what I call a 'death march' a couple of years after I moved here. I was so depressed, I literally could not see how I was going to live through the tremendous amount of pain that had infiltrated every crevice of my being. In the midst of all that pain, unexpectedly, came the most beautiful gift I had ever received. The birth of my grandson.

## Deciding to Live Again through Unconditional Love

The day Jace was born was a huge Turning Point in my life. His birth lifted me from the pain of unrequited parenthood to a love I had never experienced in my life. This new light reminded me of a beautiful, bouncy, baby bear cub, so I affectionately started calling him "Bear," and it lovingly caught on with everyone.

Little did I know, I was in for quite the surprise.

Due to some unforeseen familial issues, I ended up taking Bear under my wing after his birth. With all I had learned through my parenting mistakes and life experiences, I had come to a place spiritually where I knew if helping to raise him was going to be my role, I was determined to feed him with pure, unconditional love, allowing him to become who *he* was meant to be, not what I thought he should be. My role was to provide him the love, affection, consistency, and stewardship he deserved in order to allow his awesome star to rise. It was a powerful lesson steeped in the guilt and pain of "not knowing then what I know now," when I was raising my girls. I had unknowingly put my fears and insecurities into them, which I feel that, had I known better at the time, would have resulted in more confident, self-assured adults. I wasn't going to make the same mistake with this little life I'd been assigned to.

I had learned through the course of my spiritual evolution not to feed children your fears or beliefs, because it conditions them out of their truth.

Bear taught me the power of unconditional love. How to see life through his eyes, how to tap into my own inner child, and how to have fun again. This baby was the greatest blessing I had ever received.

When he was 4 years old, the beautiful lessons he'd taught me helped me to see that trying to build a business where I was supposed to be passionate about what I was doing (while working a job that was literally killing me) could no longer take place concurrently.

I reached the point of no return in March 2018 and decided that I'd had all I could take from my abusive employer. Even though I was making good money, I hadn't had a raise in 10 years. The money didn't matter anymore, certainly not as much as my sanity, so I walked away. Besides divorcing my husband, divorcing that j-o-b was the best *decision* I ever made in my life.

Down with the job and up with the business, I thought, at least it sure seemed that way for a while. Right after I left, a huge vortex of energy burst into my mental and physical awareness. The best way to describe it is like a tornado blew in and started inundating my life with everything I needed to take myself to the next level. In that powerful space, all the people, situations, possibilities, and opportunities showed themselves to me in rapid fashion. Holding on to that job just for the paycheck for 10 years had been holding me back from all the Universe had in store for me. The sad part is I knew it would be like that all along…but I was afraid to let go.

Again, though, despite those successes, I continued to get in my own way, held back by underlying beliefs that caused me to flatline in my professional life. In November 2019, I couldn't take it anymore…I became so depressed at not having the financial success I envisioned for my business, I decided to let it go altogether. I had evolved to a place where I felt I was flailing in space without a direction. I was broke and fatigued from trying so hard to succeed. That was the second worst bout of depression I had ever had. Why, with all the gifts that I was blessed with, was I not succeeding at living my dream?

At the turn of the New Year in 2020, through the magic of social media, I came upon a merry young band of lads and lasses from the UK whose sacred messages of manifestation and creating a life of freedom for yourself began really resonating with me. Eventually, as I attended more virtual events and was introduced to more people across their organization, I began to see new possibilities that helped me discover and finally dissolve the core belief that had been at the root of my depression for so long—the belief that I wasn't capable of earning my own living with my own business.

It was the lovely Tjibaria Pijloo of *Freedom Lifestyle Creators*™ who taught me five of the most beautiful words I had ever heard up to that point, (besides "it's a girl, Mrs. Gardner!" when my first daughter was born). She said, **"SUCCESS HAPPENS WHEN YOU DECIDE!"**

Whoa…where'd that come from? I had made decisions many times in my life, some good and some not so good. It was like a light switch immediately went off in me, and for the very first time in my half a century on this earth, I GOT IT!! Success happens when you decide that it is so. It happens when you take the time to invest in yourself, have the patience to learn, implement the steps necessary to be successful, and take the consistent action that makes it all work like a well-oiled machine.

I had finally discovered that all I needed to do was to DECIDE for success and to see myself as successful.

Now, I know my direction. I know my whole truth, and I know how to choose from a place of unconditional love for myself. I am growing a new business and lifestyle from this beautiful place I've evolved to. For the first time in my life, I acknowledge and believe that I *deserve* everything that is in my Highest Good and that I am fully capable of achieving it. All I have to do is follow through and finish the task at hand.

What path will you choose for yourself?

_____

_____

_____

_____

_____

What will you fully and completely commit yourself to?

_____

_____

_____

_____

_____

*Grown Sexy Wisdom* is the culmination of ALL that I am. It is the beautiful treasure and essence within me that I have reverse engineered to help women like you who have reached a crossroads in their lives and want to gain more clarity about a sense of purpose and direction going forward. I can help you to understand and tap into the FOUNDATION of who you are, determine where you are in your EVOLUTION and what direction you'd like to go from here. I assist with your ELEVATION by reconnecting you to the TRUTH of who you are and growing your sacred spiritual muscle, all culminating in your EMANCIPATION...creating a life of freedom, joy, and abundance that turns you ON!

*Grown Sexy Wisdom* is *me*, and it is you, too. Give yourself permission to DECIDE for yourself, to use your *GrownSexyPower* to create the life you want for yourself.

Everything you want, deserve and desire is on the other side of decision.

Isn't it time to finally make the one that will shift you into the stratosphere?

# Chapter 6

# GrownSexySecret #5:  Minding Your Sacred Energy

*"Thou shall not allow low-vibin' sketchy ass energy to penetrate thy aura!"* **– Unknown**

Ever wonder why in life you sometimes feel depressed and depleted after encounters with certain people, places, things and even situations? Wonder how you go from being happy and on top of the world one minute, but in an instant, feel the life force energy being drawn out of you when you get around a certain person or in a certain situation?

I always wondered why I'd had a lifelong battle with depression and the inability to maintain, at least for the most part, a consistently happy state of mind. After all, happiness is an inside job, but why were my insides always in an uproar? What I began to realize after much soul searching and peeling back the layers is that my lack of control over my emotional responses to people and events led me to an inability to keep my negative emotions from gaining momentum, often leading to catastrophic circumstances in my life. My brain and my body had developed these habitual 'knee jerk' responses, or 'triggers' as they're referred to in the mental health world, that automatically shifted my body, mind and spirit into a state of being that was wholly detrimental to my physical, mental, and spiritual health.

Not until Divine timing led me to the point in my journey when I began to sift and sort and become exposed to the laws of the universe through the most authentic of mentors did I open my mind to fully grasping and stepping into my knowing that we are all creative beings in every aspect of our lives. Our thoughts, beliefs, habits, and emotions take center stage in this drama we call life. Understand that everything is

106

energy and vibrates at a certain speed according to the laws of physics. The law of attraction says that 'like attracts like,' so the energy or signals you are broadcasting to the universe influence the experiences, people, and situations you attract into your life. We have a choice in every moment how to feel, what to think, and where to focus our energy, which creates our life experience. In a nutshell...we are creating our lives with every thought we think, every belief and habit we've developed, and that program is, was, and always has been creating our reality.

In setting aside the ego and getting real with myself, through prayer, meditation, and examination of my life to this point, I recently had the most profound revelation I've ever experienced. The whispers and Divine guidance I received showed me something about our beingness that I'd never thought of in quite this way before. Your sacred core energy —in other words, your heart and soul energy—is where the center of your life force energy lies. It is this sacred energy that you must be most mindful of when thinking about its effect on your life.

This core energy is needlessly expended every single day on all of those things that come up for you and trigger you toward a response that is detrimental to your life, health, and well-being. For example, a car passes you too closely on the freeway and cuts you off. The first thing you might want to do is flip the driver off, possibly even ram the back of his car, it makes you so angry. Take a second to examine how that FEELS in your body and mind in the moment it happens. Do you know how much stress you are creating for yourself and what effect it's having on you now and in the long run?

The very essence of your Divine energy and power is held

within the core or center of your beautiful being. It is indeed your *heart and soul* that you must hold most sacred. Expending this powerful Divine energy on anything that does not align with who you really are, a being of Divine love, leaves you depleted, depressed, and wandering in your circumstances versus living in the fullness and wholeness of who you truly are. It is life-changing to learn to no longer give your power away aimlessly, as doing so often leaves you resentful of yourself and of others.

Minding my sacred energy is exactly how I have healed and mended the relationship between my daughters and me. I was able to separate myself from the pain I felt, by understanding that they are beautiful just as they are. Their souls' journeys are not mine to control. I can set boundaries in order to protect myself and still love them unconditionally, without absorbing all the chaotic energy that sometimes accompanies them in their interactions with me.

Holding in reverence this sacred power and directing it in service to the world using your Divine gifts and talents and allowing yourself to live in your passion and your purpose is the energy that ignites your life and feeds your internal flame. This is the energy that transforms lives, and that will transform the world!

But how do *you* take back that sacred life force energy you just shot out there into the universe in that moment, with full-blown reactionary emotions like anger and retribution? How do you become more mindful of the negative energy you are putting out there daily and bring yourself back to center where there is balance? How do you get to that place where you don't let those types of reactions disturb your peace?

**1.) Become more SELF-AWARE of your actions and reactions in the moment that a trigger event is happening.**

Physically and mentally catch yourself immediately when something is occurring. Take a deep belly breath in through your nose and blow it out slowly through your lips, focusing on your center or core love energy. Feel the tension and reactions dissipate and melt away as you bring yourself back to your sacred center. Notice how that person who just wronged you (or 'thing' that just happened) no longer has the same significance in your field of energy.

**2.) Nurture yourself by getting grounded, and make this a consistent practice.**

If you're like me, you occasionally find yourself working so much that you forget to take time to rest your body and soul. This is when I typically get too much into my head and not enough into grounding myself so that my energy is able to vibrate in peace and harmony with the energy of the earth, which is how you keep your core energy balanced. When I want to balance my energy, all I have to do is go to my favorite beach, take off my shoes, walk in the sand, and feel the wind and blessed sun on my face. I can feel the energy of the earth coursing through my blood and into my sacred core and my mind.

What is your favorite place to go to feel at peace?

_____

_____

Where can you go to kick off your shoes, feel the earth on and in your feet, and relax your sweet soul?

_____

Do this often, and fewer and fewer things will affect you as they do when there is chaos.

**3.) Meditate, pray, journal. Release what it is you don't want and focus on gratitude and creating what you do want.**

Clearing your mind and freeing it from all the debris and toxicity that attempt to sneak in daily is something you have to be willing and open to doing. This practice will raise your vibration higher and allow you to begin to see life from a totally new perspective. The goal here is to retrain your brain toward peace and focusing on what it is that will bring joy, passion, and purpose to your life. In this space is where you can really get most in tune with your powerful core energy. From this joyful, peaceful place, we can truly allow the intentions we set forth to manifest quickly and effortlessly.

Emotions are not wrong. If you didn't allow yourself to feel them, you wouldn't be alive! There are, simply put, many beneficial ways that you can learn to manage them without letting them control your life. Learning to nurture your sacred core energy will allow you to find your 'happy' and keep the energy of joy and love at the center of your being. Holding this sacred energy and harnessing it for living your passion and purpose is the very reason you were created.

# Chapter 7

―――――◦◈◦―――――

## Driving the Message Home... Create A Life That Turns You On!

*"Across a lifetime of ups and downs, lessons and growth, you have gained the wisdom and earned the sacred right to create the next chapter of your life on YOUR TERMS!"– **Lianna Gardner***

Do that thing that sets your soul on fire! You are more than capable. You deserve it, and it is lovingly waiting for you to bring it to life! Reignite that dream that's been nipping at your heels for years, or birth a new one and ride the wave of blissful living!

Have I helped to restore your vision? Do you have more clarity around the oh so sexy, innate, and Divine magic that exists within you? YOU are a MASTERPIECE! Mastering the art of living your authentic essence is what the *Grown Sexy Wisdom* Revolution is all about. It has been my absolute pleasure in guiding you to know it, *be it* and empower you to use it!

Believe me when I tell you, the ecstasy that comes when you are in tune with the *whole* of you is one of the most beautiful things you will ever experience. All that you have been, all that you are now, and all that you are becoming is coalescing in amazing fashion. This, combined with a succinct awareness of your valuable cache of amazing gifts, skills and talents, life lessons, experiences, situational knowledge, values, and creativity, is an experience you will never forget, if you choose to live it.

I have had several moments in my life when stepping out of fear and into faith, expressing my uniqueness and living my passion, has allowed me to experience a natural high unlike any other. In that single moment, where the Divine energies of the Universe converge and *all that is you* is dancing within the manifestation of your wildest dreams, you will know it... better yet...you will feel it to your very core!

That is the *GrownSexyPower* that you possess...and this is what working your *Grown Sexy Wisdom* can do for your life.

Now that you know that the wisdom of the ages is at your fingertips…all you have to do is call it up! Live, love, laugh, and share your unique *Grown Sexy Wisdom* with others; this is your Divine birthright.

Life waits for no one. You've spent most of it pleasing and living for others, NOW is your sacred opportunity to DECIDE to create the abundance, love, health and happiness that *you* deserve.

Time is the most precious commodity you have. Once it's gone, you can never get it back. How will you choose to spend your time from this moment forward? Now that you know these 5 powerful *GrownAssSecrets* for creating a life that turns you on… don't waste another second doubting yourself or your power—put your *Grown Sexy Wisdom* to work for you! It's way past time to elevate your sexy, sassy self from ordinary to extraordinary!

Remember it is your unique vision, intention, commitment, and action that will allow the manifestation of your goals and dreams into your reality. All you have to do is practice slowing down the momentum of negative thoughts, get to know yourself better by changing your channel to focus more on your inner self, and incorporate more gratitude and happiness into your daily life. Keep your vibration high as much as possible, and the manifestation will happen more quickly.

I can't wait to see you dancing to the tune of your *Grown Sexy Wisdom* as you light your life and the world on fire… whatever path you choose!

**About the Author**

Lianna Gardner a.k.a. Lianna Empowers is a Best-Selling Author, MidlifeMENTOR, Transformational Coach, and Motivational Speaker who specializes in helping women who are at a crossroads in life gain clarity for their path forward by unlocking their unique inner power to realize the greatest version of themselves and create a life that turns them on! Lianna has successfully made the transition from living other people's narratives for her life—and putting her own dreams on the backburner—to become a successful entrepreneur. She now uses her powerful journey as a bridge to help others navigate the road toward creating the greatest chapter of their life, resulting in more love, health, abundance, and happiness than they ever thought possible. Lianna started her transformational coaching business in 2009 to help others deal with the sometimes overwhelming prospect of stepping through fear to do what they love and create their own destiny. Lianna did this herself by connecting to her inner power, overcoming limiting beliefs and poor thinking habits, starting a new business while raising two daughters, and leaving an unfulfilling job to create life on her own terms.

Lianna has spent the last 11 years as a coach, mentor, speaker and transformational workshop leader. Today, Lianna offers a wide range of programs and services—from online courses, group and individual mentoring/coaching, to seminars and motivational speeches.

To learn more about *Grown Sexy Wisdom* and how you can get started creating the greatest chapter of your life, please visit Lianna at www.liannaempowers.com, or on Facebook and Instagram: @liannaempowers, on LinkedIn at https://www.linkedin.com/in/liannagardner/ or email liannaempowers@gmail.com.